HB

D0800090

LAMBS IN BLUE

AF

Books should be returned on or before the
last date stamped below

JR
SC

ABERDEENSHIRE
LIBRARY &
INFORMATION SERVICES

WITHDRAWN
FROM LIBRARY

ABERDEENSHIRE LIBRARY
AND INFORMATION SERVICE

MEL Barnett, Rebecca RUM

Lambs in blue /
Rebecca Barnett

940.
5481 LP
1569069

A L I S
1569069

LAMBS IN BLUE

Rebecca Barnett

ISIS
LARGE PRINT
Oxford

Copyright © Rebecca Barnett, 1999

First published in Great Britain 1999
by Woodfield Publishing

Published in Large Print 2003 by ISIS Publishing Ltd,
7 Centremead, Osney Mead, Oxford OX2 0ES
by arrangement with Woodfield Publishing

All rights reserved

The moral right of the author has been asserted

British Library Cataloguing in Publication Data
Barnett, Rebecca
    Lambs in blue. – Large print ed. –
    (Isis reminiscence series)
    1. Barnett, Rebecca
    2. Great Britain. Royal Air Force. Women's Auxiliary
    Air Force 3. World War, 1939–1945 – Sri Lanka –
    Participation, Female 4. World War, 1939–1945 –
    Sri Lanka – Personal narratives, British
    5. Large type books
    I. Title
    940.5'48141'092

Barnett, Rebecc
Lambs in blue /
Rebecca Barnett
940.
5481 LP
1569069

ISBN 0–7531–9864–9 (hb)
ISBN 0–7531–9865–7 (pb)

Printed and bound by Antony Rowe, Chippenham

Foreword

A lot has been written about the men of the Royal Air Force, and rightly so. They did much for my country, England and its precious neighbours during the 2nd World War, 1939-1945.

But alongside the airmen were girls officially known as WAAFs who were doing sometimes the equal of men, though it was never asked of us to become aircrew as some Russian girls became, and who actually went out to drop bombs.

My first intent was to write pages of statistics regarding how many WAAFs served during the war, what sort of trades they were called to do, but in the end I thought that it would give a more realistic picture of what went on if I simply sat down and told my own story. The following paragraph tells why.

Some years ago a local journal in my city published a series called *What Did You Do In The War, Mummy?* and asked for local contributions. I read them and they were good, interesting.

Nevertheless I decided my own experiences were just as — in fact more — exciting. My short contribution must have raised their eyebrows to such an extent they published it in heavy type. That fact, plus remarks from acquaintances who hadn't known of my own little war made me, with over-long hindsight, realise that ours — the WAAFs' role — was not only rather vital, but funny too. I could also say that we put ourselves in danger without even realising it. Not surprising then, that on my entering the service, I remember smiling when asked for next-of-kin to be informed in case of my death.

I suppose as a female, the role of being placed in any sort of danger had not occurred to me naturally, hence the smile. I would be thinking like some very young pilots did that death was an aeon from someone of my youth. Someone like me could not even grow old.

I cannot even yet say whether life in the service made us grow up faster, or prevented us from growing up quickly enough to face the world. I can say it was an experience I suddenly knew ought to be written about, even though the writing has been so long delayed. I hope you enjoy it, and also let the story make you think of a time when a country called upon its extreme youth to save its members of all ages.

Rebecca Barnett, 1999

Contents

CHAPTER
ONE

Jean Has to Go/
Our First Lecture

Thinking back, I feel sure I was at that time quite content with my job in a manufacturer's office. I had a few nice friends there and my work was anything but boring. The "old dears" in the office at the time saw to that, and gave us young ones much cause for both anger and mirth.

One week we were all content, but the next . . .

Jean had become the problem. She'd almost reached the age to be "called up". Either she had to go and do work in an essential trade such as ammunitions, or she could "join up", go into one of the services.

I couldn't help feeling that we were already in an essential trade, as we manufactured food: jams, sauces, pickles etc. People were always blaspheming at me over the phone, trying to get more than their fair share of them, and I had to do the rationing. However, the wartime government knew what was best for us and off Jean had to go — somewhere, to do her bit because she was a little older than I was.

Jean and I used to have a sort of competition — it was to do with which of us had got the nicest compliment from a male that week — which just goes to show how young we were.

I could have accepted just Jean leaving us, but Jennie suddenly decided to go too. Now that really unsettled me. We'd been friends since we were ten and eleven, she the elder, so what could I do but agree when she said: "Come on, join up with us," on noticing my long face about it. Whether Jean had made the same suggestion to Jennie we cannot remember, but she may have done because she was a charming, home-loving girl who must at first have thought it hard to go away alone. Anyway, we were soon all excited and all going. A kind of adventurous dream had poked its way into our young minds. We were off to get revenge, for each of us had known men already killed. Our chance to do something had come.

Our bosses, the two Mr Powells, who were uncle and nephew, were quite startled at losing three of us at once, but gave us good references in spite of it. The two gentlemen wished us all good luck and the men in the bottling shed tried to frighten the life out of us with warnings.

I well remember the war starting. I was sixteen, and that day it was my mother who brought something rather serious to my attention. It was mainly the look on her face I remember as she told me "Eh dear, it's war." That's all she said then went very quiet. She would be thinking of a brother lost in the First World

2

War and of my brother too, who was eighteen months my senior.

By the time I left home I'd seen a "dog-fight" overhead. I'd heard sirens, which took me into our Anderson shelter, then I foolishly left it when I heard stuff banging outside, but realising it was dangerous "flak" I rushed back in. Other than that the war was a mystery to me, though I had filled in food ration books too, voluntarily.

The day I went home and announced "I'm going to join up" started a war, which I'd never really expected. I know now of course that although I felt very self-sufficient at eighteen, my parents did not agree.

Eighteen was the youngest I could join, and within minutes of my announcement I knew mother and father thought it still too young. The battle however, lasted in my parents' minds only. I knew I was going. It was my father who tried one last plea.

"I hope you realise you won't be able to stay out late in the army. You do as you're told when you get into that!"

I agree he must have known what he was talking about, he'd spent thirty years in it and had been the regimental sergeant major himself. I loved to go ballroom dancing in those days and was always in trouble for getting home late, though it was impossible not to as dances went on until eleven o'clock and much later sometimes.

His warning plea almost made me laugh and made absolutely no difference. That Saturday the three of us set off early for the queue at the recruiting office in town.

OUR FIRST LECTURE

"Never lend anything. And any of you who have had sex already, we advise you to come and have an examination. If you don't, and you have begun a pregnancy which has terminated itself, it will badly affect any future babies you may have when you marry."

These were just two of the blunt warnings given in a speech to a gathering, a few hundred girls strong I seem to remember, of newly recruited WAAFs by an officer who did not seem much older than the bulk of us seated there.

The woman officer would belong to "admin", I expect, and would have been briefed what to say quite carefully by a much senior officer who had in mind a bunch of innocents, which of course we were, though we'd have denied it effusively.

Our ages ranged mainly from eighteen upwards, and the majority must have been under twenty-two or three. We must also have looked all shapes and sizes, all grades of intelligence above reasonable. But they had packaged us all in blue and, seated there, only our faces and the colour of our hair gave any indication that we may have been actually more mature-minded than the "rookies" speech indicated they thought we were.

Our uniform was a near-straight skirt, long belted jacket with four pockets at the front, blue shirt, black tie, grey lisle stockings, black flat-heeled shoes. The jacket had six brass buttons, our overcoats ten, the belt a brass buckle, and our cap a brass badge. All had to be polished daily, or were supposed to be.

After the speech, not one in the audience objected to the inference that we may have had sex, or may be about to experience it. We sat there I suppose, like little lambs waiting and willing to be led, listening to advice, most of which I had not had before, nor I suspect had the others. The farthest I'd been taken was to be shown the picture of a baby being born when I'd been a Ranger.

We had no television in those days to open wide our eyes regularly to the wickedness of things and people. We knew only what our parents had or hadn't told us, and most hadn't; or else had garbled it so well we hadn't understood its meaning. The authorities of course knew all this, but they too should have treated us as adults and simply said: "Promiscuous girls get babies, and sometimes V.D."

Their attitude reminded me of the pamphlet my doctor had handed me when my mother told him I had started "bleedings". The pamphlet delicately but falsely informed me that the bleeding was another way of the body cleansing itself of impurities. Adult intelligence had not advanced much by 1941, I felt, as I listened to the initiation speech.

Thank heavens our own natural intelligence was the thing that really guided us, or most of us, safely through the next few years, plus the fact that all servicemen too had been guided as to sex and told what to use if they must have it.

The immediate future was indeed to be surrounded by temptations, away from our homes, suddenly close-knit to a large community of strangers, though some became friends never to be forgotten. The war was to pull a heavy curtain across our lives, thrust us into new adventures, for whereas in the normal circumstances of those days, we young women would have been "being prepared" in domestic achievements for the most likely of trades for us then, marriage for the girls, we'd been suddenly uprooted from all that and had gone just like the boys "to win the war".

My own example of how I came to leave the fold and join our new roles so willingly must have been repeated many times across the land in those unsettling days for both young and old.

As I said, we had to join at a recruiting office, which I don't remember very well. We were all probably too nervously excited for that. I do remember the old boy that medically examined us. Certainly, he was a white-haired fatherly type, but being eighteen I could not imagine why he "weighed" my bosoms with his hands as part of the health-check.

As a female, I was well aware these things come in all weights, but thought they had nothing to do with good or bad health like stomachs. If only he'd explained the weighing! And of course I was already praying I would turn out A1, fit to become an airwoman. Anyway, there was no mention of them later on the leaflet in my Royal Air Force service book either weight-wise or anything.

It simply said, date of birth, height, marks and scars (which were nil), and perhaps that's what he'd been looking for. I was rather an uninteresting specimen it appeared. It seemed I was as healthy as I'd always felt and they let me in.

As I'd been working in an office and could already type, it was said I should join as a teleprinter operator. No ifs or buts, they just seemed to need me immediately. Lamb-like I accepted the non-discussed trade as had Jean and Jennie. I didn't even know what a teleprinter was and nobody in life had encouraged me to ask questions. It never occurred to me to ask for a list of occupations available. Now I think I'd like to have been in transport. I think if they'd suggested we become ablution cleaners we'd have agreed, after a slight hesitation. Youth willingly strides the bounds of insanity almost.

It took just a few weeks for the big day to arrive, and without so much as even a joke about them, the three of us left our boyfriends almost weeping in the village square. For a change the girls were leaving the boys behind. It must have made them think a lot in the next few weeks, one especially I knew who later became vitally involved in my life. He looked stunned as I said a short "Goodbye".

Our future stretched before us akin to the dreams of all those young beauties of that era that dreamed of such things as the "Hollywood Trail". Our trailings though were to be vastly different from that kind of dream. It was to turn out more like "back to the woods" for us.

And it had all started as we'd stood grouped in the office I remember making what seemed the greatest decision of our lives. Which of the three main services to join? Army, Navy, or Air Force. The decision had been unanimous almost immediately. It had to be the Air Force.

There was only one stumbling block to that. Jean never wore blue. She was a startling red-head, and up until then, blue was unthinkable in her wardrobe. But blue it became; yet as clothes conscious as I was in those days, I have no idea what each wore as we waited to board the train for Gloucester. I only know that our mothers had come along too to see us off and were in tears. Jean's mother ceremoniously handed us a silver threepenny bit each, for luck, she said. We made a promise to keep them while we were away. I really cannot remember what happened to the object of my promise, and I cannot recall having much luck in the years I was to be parted from everyone I knew.

Others at the time it has been revealed to me would have given a lot to be in our place at that station. As one lady told me as I was researching for this: "I also went with two friends to become a WAAF. Both my friends passed their medical but I had a burst eardrum so the Air Force didn't want me. I almost got a burst heart too for I cried all that night. Undeterred, next week I went to try and join the Army, but found myself faced with the same medical examiners. It never occurred to me that the same medical team operated for all of the services. I wept even more, but however I got some consolation. I eventually went away to work and found myself concerned with the Frank Whittle team, the jet man. I got my excitement in the end. You might even say I became one of the Jet-Set!"

Another lady told me she eagerly chucked a civil service post that was classed as essential work and never regretted it. She went back to it after the war. She remembered being put in charge of about three dozen new recruits at the railway station before she ever got into uniform.

I was aware that the Royal Air Force was a highly organised service before the war, but the more I have learnt the more I have been amazed at the administrative skill it must have taken to run smoothly so many recruits in so many trades.

The records office must house some of the most exciting or dramatic details of British history. Events of the Battle of Britain alone should thrill or shock for many decades anyone who delves into them. In fact I think it was the courage of aircrew then, a new kind of courage from that we were used to in the Navy, that inspired many to join the ranks of blue. Cinema newsreels had formed a sort of backbone to our young dreams.

We left home in September 1941 from the Central Station, Newcastle-upon-Tyne. We left our mothers sad and our fathers thoughtful, I think. After all they'd already had a war but were now too old. I was never able to ask my father why he appeared so worried that I was now going to war.

CHAPTER TWO

Gloucester and Morecambe

Although we had started off with the pleasing idea that we would all be going away together, we had not given a thought to becoming separated eventually. However, in the first instance we were called upon to train ourselves via various methods to become army-minded.

What exactly this was meant to achieve, or whether it achieved exactly what it meant, I don't know, but I sensed a similarity to knowledge I had formed of a men's army, where commands and marching instil a sense of discipline into its unsuspecting beings. A WAAF even had to fasten her coats across from left to right, but both sexes took belts the other way.

Gloucester was, or seemed, a shock. Not that we ever saw anything of Gloucester itself, and we were there only a short time, which was more than enough. My memory was of feeling cold, eating dreadful food, and worst of all having to attempt to wash our "tools" (knife, fork and spoon) after we'd eaten, in a very large tank of water outside. The water looked cold and grease patterns floated on and through it, so that in the end I started to wash mine under the tap of the wash-basins. Having already had strong advance warnings of punishments dished out for any offences seen, I did this little act in fear and trepidation that I could get jankers or maybe shot if caught, so I made sure I wasn't, and this awareness attached itself to me on many occasions during the one thousand, five hundred and sixty six days I served my country.

The other main Gloucester memory was of standing in a queue, taking turns to sit on wooden chairs, and allowing a white-uniformed nurse to lift our hair strands one at a time to look for "the gallopers" — nits or lice. The poor blushing souls who weren't free of them we knew about, for they were left behind a little longer until they were. I really blessed my mother then for making me fine-tooth-comb myself so regularly at home. I escaped thankfully to Morecambe where we had to begin our footslog.

Things looked brighter from the beginning at Morecambe. It had really taken a very short time to "sign on" and actually get into uniform. It seems that most of us had our photograph taken within the first days of wearing it, and a copy always went home, though the act was not deliberate on anyone's part. Photographers — the kind who snap you along the promenade anywhere you care to holiday — were already there, eagerly awaiting each new innocent batch to arrive. Each ex-WAAF I've spoken to had one taken, often looking rather surprised at the unexpectedness of the click, looking very very young, yet also aware of the rules and regulations another lecture had informed us

11

about. Our coats were correctly buttoned, our peaked hats at as straight an angle as our pride would allow, our buttons already gleaming, and shoes shining.

As it was cold weather when we were there, my photo shows us all wearing thick woollen Air Force blue gloves too. We were also showing the strap across our chests of our gas-masks in a case as we strode purposefully along the clean Morecambe pavement. We had been three for the cameraman and were giggling girlishly through our surprise.

As was typical throughout our service, we often used the others with whom we were billeted as friends. It was too convenient not to. We were all "rookies" there and would have felt very lonely trying to go it alone in any sense.

The war had caused a mass movement of people in the British Isles, and all had to be housed in some way, somewhere, which would be the reason Morecambe had been one of the places chosen while we were being readjusted and organised into a workable mass.

The normal seaside season was over for the Morecambe landladies who handled the summer crowds, so it was ideal that they should have their beds and bedrooms put to good use on behalf of the war effort. In any case the beaches themselves were closed to everyone for the duration because of mines danger. For the whole period there I shared a smallish room with two other WAAFs. We had a single bed each, in a typical clean boarding house of those days. The bedding was smooth, cheerful and warm, and a bedside lamp cheered us before we switched off for sleep after laughing about the day's events. We were usually so tired, that before sleep there were no small moments for homesickness. Outside our knowledge, it was to be the last comfortable bedroom we'd enjoy for four years or more — apart from going home on leave.

My two bedroom friends were both Cockneys, the first I'd ever met; though I was to meet more of them later in my home, as evacuees. We really did not have time to get to know each other well. From the moment we arose at daybreak our time was mapped out. It was breakfast first in our digs followed each day by marching, exercising and lectures.

The marching, in the end, did what it was supposed to I'm sure. It smartened us up physically, those who needed it doing. The good sea air helped us in that measure. The marching also gave us a pride in our uniform, because we learnt to be "on show" as they routed us from one spot to another.

There were casualties to routine of course, as in all walks of life. I was one almost immediately. I got a poisoned finger somehow and for two or three days had to attend sickbay to get it looked at and dressed. I was ordered to catch my lot up always and spent a considerable amount of time running around streets trying to catch sight of my own particular caterpillar of WAAFs.

We had been taught we must salute at each officer seen, and I remember between running to catch my lot having to pull myself up to a smart walk for the salute on greeting every one. Either there were a lot of officers or because of my running round in circles I may have been meeting the same one, but my cheeks felt forever red with exertion of one kind or another.

They must have wanted to make absolutely sure we were quite fit before sending us off to our varied courses, because at Morecambe they stripped us to our underwear around the edge of the open-air pool near the beach, for exercises under the benevolent-looking eyes of an RAF bod (bod always being used to refer to another human in forces language which consisted of many strange terms, we were to discover).

One day also, we were obliged to experience a gas-raid. They used the real stuff, for two or three bods were in the gas chamber trying to hurry us through as we lined up in turn. It was a slightly alarming thought for me because my father had suffered from the gas effects he caught during the first World War. He coughed a great deal each morning on waking because of it.

Thankfully, they forgot about us in the evenings and were probably sipping away to their own hearts' content in some hotel. By then the fresh air and exercise we were all suffering had us quite ravenous. But even then they guided us, told us of the gathering spots where we might buy snacks if we wished, and the RAF men were obviously told of the same places. I expect they hoped that if we were going to try and meet the opposite sex while let loose, they would prefer us to meet the ones they had already examined!

We found ourselves most evenings inside this large building into which were crammed masses of blue uniforms. I remember it mainly for its smoky

14

atmosphere and standing room only. The air, what was left of it, was so blue that our new uniforms paled against it. What benefit all those miles of marching?

We arrived there in small bunches, and each bunch would glance at, and be given glances from the opposite sex bunches, but all the warnings we'd had must have been holding us back.

I do remember though going to a cinema one evening with Jennie and Jean and some RAF bods, one of whom was a Welshman who found our accents new to him, as did the other two from the Midlands. We all gradually came to meet all our nationals, all the many accents from Britain. Each accent was usually scoffed at, but always only in the friendliest manner.

The days passed quickly, and though we were all still Athenas, still on a feminine roundabout, we were in some respects beginning to feel like soldiers. The slang of forces language helped to raise us in a large sense from what had been a more timid role, previously, I think. We shouted "wakey-wakey!" in the mornings, talked of a "pukka lot" or of things being a "wizard prang" and everybody was simply a "bod".

We left Morecambe feeling mightily refreshed, fully-fledged in the manners of the Air Force and quite ready for whatever was ahead, be it fair or foul — and in truth it turned out both.

The two Cockneys went off "somewhere" to become mechanics, while Jean, Jennie and I were moved to Cranwell, I to experience my first Air Force romance, as no doubt did many others.

Meanwhile, we knew nothing whatever of what was going on in the War. I suppose with our new-found life we'd forgotten all about the reason why we'd found it, as well as never coming within earshot of a radio and the 9 o'clock news.

It is interesting enough to mention that at one lecture, the officer requested that anyone able to identify aircraft of our own or enemy makes should raise a hand. Although a few hundred were seated, not a hand went up, although the audience was made up of as many men as girls. We must all have been of the one intelligence — if it was dropping bombs it was an enemy plane. It seemed clear at that point that we all had a lot to learn.

CHAPTER
THREE

Cranwell

Having completed the initiation lectures and foot slogging, we had now arrived at Cranwell to learn our trade. As my enquiries have proved, our trades were mostly chosen for us. I explained how it happened at my own recruitment centre, and that explanation seems to duplicate what happened elsewhere with most others.

One ex-WAAF did not surprise me when she also stated, just as I have done, "If I'd had a choice I would have liked to have been in transport". When I told her "Me too," she gave me a look of fellow understanding of something lost and all too late now anyway.

She had actually been sent on a crash six-week accountancy course. Their accountancy covered every item dealt with at their particular unit. Food and clothing for each of the personnel and equipment for whichever service of the force they were running. It could have been a barrage-balloon unit, or an operational flying station, or the headquarters of some group. Or even the RAF Records Office itself, which was an enormous concern where a large card held every movement of every person in the Air Force. It is therefore true to say that WAAFs had a finger in most things. Perhaps in a future war, which heaven forbid, they will like Russian women, drop bombs also.

How our women were eventually asked to fly aircraft came about when it was decided that precious flying hours were lost simply ferrying aircraft between various stations, at a time when there was a shortage of combat pilots. I one day saw the notice on a board asking for WAAFs interested in doing the job. It was a while after I'd settled into my own trade. Here at last I thought was something just up my street and I was straight off to see an officer.

I felt a little heartbroken when they did not send for me, follow up my volunteering, I was so sure they'd be desperate for me. As usual though they decided in the end what they wanted of you or thought you capable of. Anyway the ferrying blossomed into a very useful service and solved some problems.

Cranwell, in a sense could be termed one of the hearts of the Air Force. My first impression was that it was nicely situated in the Lincolnshire countryside. Its main purpose was for the turning out of RAF officers, which did not include we who were training for our role as "Signals" personnel of the lowest ranks. Yet in a sense too we were all apprentices there, and it was at Cranwell that we felt the taste of real discipline.

The Cranwell College buildings were quite splendid ones really, and we were fortunate here to be housed in good redbrick ones, though that was the limit of our luxury, apart from a small electric fire.

18

We had the good old issue blankets now, a dull grey colour, which had to be folded each morning, and made up into a bed each night. And we had to be in our quarters by ten o'clock sharp. We started the ritual there, which went on through our service lives. This was kit-inspection, which was held each week, when we would have to display all our Air Force issue in a certain way on top of our bed, all in regulation cleanliness.

It was dark November when we arrived at Cranwell and again I have a memory of cold chills about us a lot of the time. We seemed to do a lot of marching to our allotted classrooms in darkness, or perhaps returning from them.

Again we formed "crocodiles", and a funny memory is that the last WAAF of the "croc" was given a lamp to carry during darkness. Yet the crocodiles were one of the most exciting times at Cranwell, for it was while marching we were able to sum up the "talent" amongst the crocodiles of RAF apprentices as they in the same way were eyeing us. Many a shy or bold smile crossed the narrow space between us, for all crocodiles seemed to emerge about the same time and pass at the same spot daily, almost crashing into each other. Many of these apprentices were from the lands of the Commonwealth such as Australia, from which country those boys looked handsomely attired in a uniform of much darker blue which made the wings of their trade much more striking. There was, and there still is, no doubt that a uniform can transform a person. Whereas one might imagine that a uniform makes like of each person, in fact it pulls the individuals apart, for it accentuates the face, which in truth radiates a person's soul.

Again, Jennie and Jean and I were separated as to billets and even classrooms, but we were able to meet in the evenings. It was at Cranwell that I met a new friend, a Yorkshire girl with shining fair hair and true peaches and cream complexion, who in fact was occasionally referred to as "The Palmolive Girl" because of her lovely skin. I will refer to her as Valerie. I have decided to rename some of my WAAF acquaintances because there are stories to tell which may cause embarrassment. Yet in truth there should be no need for such, for we were all at that tender age, being often led into as well as learning about life. Learning it in the process of being a WAAF is no different from learning it elsewhere, wherever girls may be at such an age.

In actual fact we more often than not never referred to one another by Christian names. Every service person started and finished his or her service life as a number and I've never met anyone yet who cannot remember it. It slides off their tongue as easily as their own name.

On wages parade each week for example we would form lines and stand at ease. The order would then come for each person, such as "2568 Brown". Brown would snap to attention, march forward to a desk where they would verify the correct Brown by his full number, (mine had seven digits) and only then pay him.

An "Admin" (administration person) wishing to contact us about anything would simply call us out by surname, so that we too got into the habit of referring to one another likewise. It seemed the natural thing to do, or was otherwise a reminder of what we'd got ourselves into, but there was no offence in it at all. But I, in ode to past and good friendships, will use Christian names.

At Cranwell we would visit one another's house and perhaps we would attend the station dance together or go for a snack to the "NAAFI", an organisation which provided us with small necessities to make our life bearable. And we would sometimes simply walk about, for that had been a great pastime of Jennie and myself. We'd often "hiked" in pre-war days.

One evening we were strolling and came upon a group of Australian boys with whom we stopped to talk. They of course had made the opening remark and before long we were in earnest conversation. They had not been long in England, so were naturally full of comment about conditions here at that exact time. They commented on the lack of variety in food they were enduring, mentioning that they never seemed to see fruit or sweets.

"Fruit!" we cried, almost in unison, "What's that?"

The small crowd in dark blue glanced at one another as if in disbelief, or perhaps shock at real belief.

"Wait a minute," they told us, and two disappeared. In a minute or two they reappeared. One of them handed us a large tin of something, which was already opened, and at the same time handed us a large spoon.

We tentatively peered into it in the extreme darkness and it was the smell rather than what we were able to see which made Jennie call out "Good Lord!" There was a verifying second, then she almost screeched: "They're peaches!" It was a case of "to heck with the spoon" when all our fingers dived instantly into the really large tin of really beautiful peaches, and I think the young Aussies were quite overcome at seeing our pleasure. I can still taste those peaches as I write about it!

We attended our teleprinter classes daily. These were machines rather like typewriters, but electrical; and they formed a secret network of lines for sending signals during the war, because the lines could not be tapped.

One strange incident I remember well. We had learnt all we were expected to and were about ready to go out and do the real job, but of course we had to pass our examination as in any trade.

One day we were lined up along our machines and told: "This is a test", and urged to give of our very best concentration, which we did. Then a few days later we were told: "Today you are getting your examination proper. You'll be taken out one by one."

My turn came, and while walking along, a RAF Sergeant told me: "Right, your turn now. However, I'm pleased to tell you that you've already passed. You passed on your test the other day. We did it that way to give you all a fair chance. Anyway, you're all getting a further chance. You were just two words short from achieving a pass as ACW1. See if you can manage it."

We arrived at the examination room. He looked at me and then spoke, looking rather apologetic as he did: "I'm sorry, but this is the only machine available, but don't be nervous and just do your best. As I've told you, you've already passed. We just want you to do better."

I sat down at the machine which stood on its own, but, it was placed facing a whole classroom of young RAF men also sitting at teleprinters, and obviously, according to the slowness of their tapping, just newly learning the trade.

It was enough to give any young woman the jitters, and in those sex-segregating days, even in the Air Force, boys and girls trained in separate rooms to be teleprinter operators. I hardly need say that I did not get those two extra words in. My fingers started off like bits of jelly, and for the time being I remained ACW2.

Yet I came off better than Valerie. As she explained to me afterwards: "I fell off the stool in a dead faint." And that's exactly what she had done, although she had already passed also. Perhaps it had been their way of seeing how well we could work under stress, of a bombing raid, or in the middle of some sort of upheaval which of course had already been happening in England.

Christmas fell upon us while we were at Cranwell, our first away from home, so of course the three of us felt we had to take some sort of action to make the best of it somehow. Our folks, bless them, had sent what little luxuries the war was allowing them, and Jean was particularly boasting and offering to share her jar of caviar which a good aunt had sent her.

It was arranged where we would all meet, and we picked a rather late hour for our party. We'd dug a Christmas tree, quite unofficially from somewhere outside camp as best we could with a knife and much heaving, which we decorated with the strangest objects a Christmas tree must have ever seen! I had to leave my billet in the secrecy of the dark and remember having a terrible time trying to cross the railway lines in the pitch-black. I bent clinging to the cold steel rails in case I fell and was glad to meet up with Jennie.

It wasn't only the crossing of the lines that had bothered me, but I was also in absolute agony with great blisters on my heels, so that I was walking half in and half out of my shoes. Jennie was also having foot trouble and hers had got so bad she had to seek medical advice, and they gave her permission to get back to her civvie shoes until her feet had healed again. Our shoes were made from grand, solid black leather, fit to walk through any mire, but until our feet had got used to them, there's no other way to say it: "By God, they hurt!" Yet get used to them our feet somehow did, but speaking personally, I was never able to wear smart female high-heels ever again after the war. Over four years in flatties saw to that.

I didn't get caught for being late out for the party, and we felt like boy scouts must at their first camping out. But there were times when we were suddenly checked to make sure we were in our billets.

24

One night, another WAAF I knew thought she would probably be late back in, and as she had no special pass she asked me would I stand in for her in case of an officer's inspection. Sporting-like, or fool-like, I agreed to take the risk.

The officer did come round, and to cover up for Pat, I had to dash from her room as soon as the officer left and deviously work my way to the side of my own bed as the officer angled in and out of other rooms. The only reason we could get away with tricks like that was that we had barely any light in our rooms. On reflection, I think the electric bulb must have been a twenty-five watter, it was always so dark at night, so that the officer would have had to be very observant or have feline eyes to notice the same person in two places.

Of course the reason for the poor lighting was to ensure blackout regulations. We were all so young, and the young are notoriously careless, even about things that matter. They couldn't risk bright lights becoming unveiled by anyone, even briefly, where so many personnel were at risk, in case enemy aircraft appeared. Therefore at night when we had to wash and set our hair it was quite a struggle and things like letter writing or sewing were difficult. Pat left me a bag of sweets on my pillow as a thank-you a few days later.

We felt relaxed enough at Cranwell also to take in a little romance. We paired off more than we had since leaving home. My own first Air Force romance began at the camp dance one night. I was still quite a shy person then, and found myself sitting on a side-seat when a boy in uniform of course, himself looking equally shy, turned and smiled and said a gentle "Hello". I smiled back and then noticed the word "Poland" at the top of his sleeve. We sat together for a few dances after that and danced now and then. His English though was very poor, almost nil, but he would struggle and try. But I was very impressed, as young people easily are, one night, when he told me: "You are just like the girls in books about England." How did he know when his English was so poor? Of course perhaps he'd read a translation, or seen a film. Anyway I swallowed it, and all its romantic implications.

He walked me "home" each time and at the end bowed his "Goodnight". Then came the night he sat and jerked out to me with difficulty the message that he had to leave Cranwell next day. He looked heartbroken as he told me. As usual he began to walk me home and on the way we had to pass by some huts. Quite suddenly he turned and grabbed me, and with determined force slipped me with him to the side of a hut. He began to unleash enough passion and in such a manner that would worry most young ladies. He used the simple manner of biting at my ear, but it was when his good white teeth really rather began to hurt I tore myself from him and fled; though I managed a sympathetic "Goodbye" to him. It was the end of my romance, and put me off Poles for the rest of the war. I'd never been aware that biting of the ear was a romantic gesture. In fact, biting of any sort was out for me.

Of course I had to tell Jennie and the others if only to relieve my surprise at his sudden swoop, whereupon they all fell into fits of giggles. I apologise here and now if the young Polish man was being sincere. Perhaps his book heroines had succumbed too easily. Perhaps he adored small ears. But at eighteen years, violence is not acceptable even in the mildest form. Gentleness would have won me much better.

While at Cranwell, we got our first real yearning for adventure in respect of moving about to see places we had not seen; and of course Lincoln being so close to Cranwell, we went there. It even seemed exciting just gazing into the shops there, and as we had not spent much money so far, we had all accumulated several pounds. Being confined to camp for so long had brought us that benefit anyway, and we enjoyed our first café meal.

Then I splashed out and bought myself my first good watch. In a way it was an act of trying to retain my femininity. It was the only sort of jewellery, if a watch may be called that, which we were allowed. The watch had a gold case but the feminine part of me had particularly admired the mother-of-pearl face on it and it cost me just over five pounds.

Thereafter however, we most of us always seemed to be short of money, once we had started travelling about. It was a case of either staying in camp where there was really little comfort to be found, or going out somewhere, which nearly always costs money. It was probably the reason why we were supposed to be so hard up in the forces. In actual fact, considering we got

27

free bed and board and clothing, the money we got was really all pocket-money, but it took a lot of that to keep us happy out of camp. And lots of us sent some money home too. A few shillings extra meant a lot to some families in those days unless they'd got into "munitions".

Talking of money reminds me of a friend called Ricky. She was trying to find her new station one day. She asked two housewives could they tell her. "No," they said. Not surprising, it was hidden in the middle of a pit-heap, she said; but anyway, one of the ladies offered to keep her kit bag until she found it while the other offered her a shilling. "Here pet, in case you have to get a bus." Ricky tells me: "I took the shilling, but couldn't risk leaving the kit bag. We were always desperate for money. I remember once we were so fed up we tried to sneak into a cinema. We asked if we could use the ladies, which was inside the ticket door. The usherette let us go in. We bravely strode into a seat after we came out, but I'm afraid she wasn't so dim. She came and yanked us out but instead of kicking us out altogether she found us a cheap seat. Even half-price entry didn't stretch our wages far enough."

Kit bags, as Ricky had reminded me, were quite a burden for slim young girls and looked rather enormous to someone of five-foot size with no muscle. They were hoisted aloft on a shoulder or alternatively dragged in the dirt. It would have been tantamount to mutiny to lose one. Ricky found her camp by at last spotting a RAF Sergeant, and had him laughing about the spot of charity she'd been handed. I've just learnt on research that kit bags were eventually made with handles for carrying, but that must have been after I went east for I never ever saw one.

The day came when we left Cranwell behind, but before going on to a permanent base where our real work would begin, we were allowed home on leave. I arrived home minus the make-up pouch I'd left home with. It had contained about six or seven tubes of lipstick of varying shades, because I had always been careful to match my lipstick to my outfit before joining up. I'd lost it, in Lincoln, left in a powder room somewhere I imagine. Anyway it had lost its importance for me now that I was almost permanently in blue. I stuck mainly to the fashionable cyclamen shade from then on. Jennie had thought it important to take away with her a small satin-covered blue address book, not only because it contained vital information but also because she liked it. She managed not to lose that. When Jennie and I went on our first leave, we were drawn to go back and visit the small dance hall where we'd learnt ballroom dancing. We were greeted warmly on our return, and managed to win an all ladies' foxtrot competition that night. The "all ladies" idea was mirroring the fact that young men were beginning to look scarce on the home front. We went wearing our uniforms and the MC made the comment: "Well, they've certainly shown us the way to come home." We won five shillings apiece. I think it was the last time we ever went there. We got the feeling after that that we'd outgrown the place.

However, two of the boys we'd left behind who were still going to the dance regularly asked to escort us home. We agreed, but were furious on the walk when they suggested we pair off and have sex. We couldn't believe our ears!

"Oh," they apologised, though rather too mildly we thought, "we thought girls in uniform didn't object to that sort of thing." We were not only furious but also so embarrassed we didn't lower ourselves to ask what had given them that idea. We just hurried off and left them, glad of the daunted look we'd left them with, and muttering about young men who weren't away in the army anyway.

The one thought dominating our minds that week though, was not what other people should be doing, but where we would be sent to ourselves. The postman would deliver the khaki communication with the exciting information in time for us to return to a whole new set of adventures. By then though, we realised we would not necessarily be given the same destination on our new posting. And already the few months we'd had in different houses with complete strangers had broken the spell of our friendship. Nevertheless we kept our fingers crossed.

CHAPTER
FOUR

Train Voucher to Kimberley

My posting order came quickly by post as I'd expected, and I eagerly opened up the contents. My mother was just as anxious as she stood by me. "Kimberley! That's in South Africa!" she exclaimed, after I'd read the directive.

Unhappily for me it wasn't. We discovered England also had one. I imagined going to Africa, but my Kimberley was in the heart of my country, or near enough. However, I'd never been to Nottinghamshire, and I remembered only from school days that lace was made there. A far cry from the diamonds of South Africa's Kimberley.

In fact Kimberley was the spot where I had to take the train to. The camp was a little distance beyond that. I'd been posted to HQ No. 12 Group which also belonged to Fighter Command. I discovered that after I'd got there.

Jennie rushed to me with her news soon after that. She had been posted to an operational station in Lincolnshire. I'd got the softest option, but I only realised this on visiting her some time later, after I'd spent months thinking she was living up to her neck in excitement.

There was, in fact, no standard domicile for WAAFs. Some were billeted with civilian families, some lived in Nissen huts (a kind of corrugated iron erection), oh, all sorts of buildings were used to house us. There was some moaning about the conditions some of us experienced, but we probably would have considered ourselves lucky if we knew of those that soldiers and others lived in. Those who were glad for survival alone perhaps, in tents maybe, both on and under snow, and other such appalling conditions. Some hadn't even a tent, like those who kept moving on in the jungle, where I eventually landed myself. And sailors weren't exactly in luxury either. Bunks perhaps, but, oh dear, the danger! As I also was to discover.

Where Jean went for that first posting I never got to know. She lived a few miles distant and few people had phones then. But when I managed by sheer luck to contact her in regard to writing this book, I learnt she had in fact also been to HQ 12 Group, but after I'd left unfortunately. She went to many camps; ten I think.

Even though our posting seemed so important, it was not guaranteed we'd remain stable. As one WAAF recalls: "We lived in Nissen huts, but there was so much commotion from Irishmen doing civilian work in the camp, for safety's sake they moved us out and let the Irish into the huts. We went into the church hall, and that was worse than the huts; no thanks to the Lord." Some WAAFs were even put into hotels. It was apparently the luck of the draw where we lived, and how we lived.

At HQ I lived in a good solid hut, which resembled a hospital ward of those days, long and very public. In winter we kept the two huge coke stoves blazing, and we had brown linoleum on the floor which we ourselves had to keep highly polished along with window cleaning and bed making. The floor reminds me of one week when we had the usual officer inspection. We had all been highly complimentary to one another because the floor looked immaculate. It shone so well, that we were admiring our own reflections almost. When the officer appeared, she tore us apart quite ruthlessly about the state of it. We didn't dare of course, but we were gasping to ourselves: "The rotten so-and-so. She wants to get her specs cleaned!" I felt like handing her the tin of Mepo which is what we cleaned our windows with, as well as our buttons. It took off paint, rust and everything. We also had a laundry to do our washing.

One of the more unpleasant tasks we had came up at intervals only thank goodness, when we'd find ourselves on the notice board in the hut for the specific job. Then there'd be great guffaws from the others: "Ha-ha Smith, it's your turn for S.T.s!" Then two of us would have to take them and stuff them into the huge mad-hot boiler used for heating the bath and wash-water. We would give a shiver of success at the end of it, to watch the sanitary towels disappear.

I've little memory of the actual food we got, as some people seem to take a delight in remembering, except that I know it wasn't spectacular in the sense of enjoying it. One morning though stands out. It was written on the notice board in almost flamboyant letters: "Pancakes with lemon". My juices mounted for breakfast as I gazed at the magic words. I adored pancakes with lemon. It reminded me of home on cold mornings in the glow of the hearth. I liked them swimming with juice.

I lined up gladly that morning only to reach a WAAF who was actually using an eye-dropper. She counted out two drops of lemon-juice. I sincerely hoped the ship that brought them did not get blasted in any way on its return to lemon-land. It honestly wasn't worth it.

I do remember there was nearly always jam on the table for tea. This brought an abundance of wasps in summer the way it does in careless cafés. A brunette friend of mine took great delight in chopping the unwary ones in two with a swipe of her knife, which to me did not seem lady-like, and particularly as she'd informed me she'd been to boarding school until recently. She'd been finished off, she told me laughing, which seemed to me they'd simply given her the guts to do things I couldn't. Many things she did later cemented that idea I ended up with about her. She was also already married and just nineteen. Yet I liked the girl, and also envied the fact she was not shy like me.

Occasionally we were made to eat in the fields. Of course it was war and that necessity could have come about had we been invaded. I defy the description of the dinners we would then get. They were pencilled up as stew, but even the midges, which came in happy groups, took one look and left. Yet I happily remember the breakfasts I enjoyed after doing night shift. Our job was a twenty-four hour one. Then we'd get bacon and eggs as if in reward for the night we'd put in.

Apart from camp meals we always seemed to be trotting up and down the paths to and from the NAAFI. Tea was my weakness, and we'd buy it in large pots. That was probably one of our luxuries in life.

Happily for me, Valerie, my fainting friend from Cranwell, also landed at HQ 12 Group. We were taken in tow almost immediately by Ross, the boarding school one who hailed from Southport, but now had a home near Liverpool since her marriage.

A number of WAAFs gained nicknames almost immediately too, which was sometimes all we ever knew them by. Ross is what I've called the impish brunette who got up to some quite naughty tricks and seemed to involve everyone else in them. But everyone in the hut seemed to mix together well, though we mostly all worked shifts and did various things with various people.

We had to have special passes to get into the operations building and keeping secrecy of our work, the messages we received and sent, was strongly emphasised to us. We had to pass armed Air Force Police to get into the building, and even though I later got to know one of them very well personally, he still would not let me pass without my showing him the permit.

Despite it being wartime, there was still plenty of snobbery about. There was a sort of rest room where we split numbers on night shift. It meant we were all available for emergency, but half of us would lie down to sleep, then change over halfway through the shift, onto the machines. We did the lying down on the floor, one grey blanket, and no pillow. I still remember the stiffness on waking.

It was in this room that we, the signals bunch, came face to face with the plotters, those who worked on the round operations table with the officers above them in the gallery. They often had noticeable upper-crust accents and the sort of manner that went with it. The whole of their talk came across as upper crust too.

After the war I had a dentist whose daughter, who was also his receptionist, had been one of them. When he knew I'd been a WAAF too he told her. We had actually worked in the same building once. She made nothing of the fact while her father filled my teeth causing me to be silent, so later I also refrained from making any recall. Some of them seemed to have a flair for exhibitionism, but perhaps that was just imagination, yet it was not only my opinion. On the other hand, we, the signals lot, put ourselves above some trades too. We were all wrong of course.

It was agreeable to us that as signals personnel we could wangle our way out of things like "church parade" or "PT" (physical training). As one WAAF recalls: "At our camp we kept changing our religion every week. One week we were Catholics, the next Protestant, and even Jehovah got his chance!"

It was true that many of us slipped out of the habit of church-going as soon as we left home. Perhaps a trick one WAAF did to me just after I arrived at HQ cured me. She just came up to me and said would I care to go to church. I agreed with a vague sort of feeling. I hardly knew her, but off we went. However, as soon as the service finished, she turned and said: "Just a minute, will you?" She then crossed the aisle to some people and began to talk to them. In a few minutes she returned while I had been left wondering what her urgency was about. She then said: "I hope you don't mind, but I've been invited to someone's house." I must have given her a funny look and off she strode again.

I was beginning to discover there were some rather strange people, even if they did go to church. Why hadn't I been asked? I didn't have horns; I knew every hymn, every prayer. I was very smart. Why had she asked me to go to church then!

I had a nasty let-down feeling as I walked back alone to camp, and by a church crowd of all people. It was my first puzzled observation of adult churchgoers. I have become more and more puzzled by religion since.

Of course some girls did keep it up. One ex-WAAF told me: "Oh yes, I kept it up. I liked going. In fact I was sent on a leadership course." Then she went on to tell me of the smashing time she'd had at her camp. "I had a great boyfriend there," she said, then added in more of a whisper, "of course he was married, but you know what they were!" As an afterthought she said, "Eh, weren't we young and innocent!" I smiled, thinking of my book's title.

Generally speaking, all the girls I was with were really great. Great fun, great-hearted, great to live with, there was so much natural fun. But there were misfits. In one hut I've been told about, two of its inmates caused a great deal of embarrassment to the rest. So much so, the rest complained to the Sergeant, who in turn must have complained to an officer. The two lesbians — something most of us hadn't a clue about — were got rid of and separated. The intention for a high standard in the service was looked at quite closely, fortunately.

One day our bunch did get roped in to do PT.

"Right, you lot," said the Sergeant, "this is one time you're not getting out of it! Follow me." She led us across to the tennis courts in bloomers and shirts.

It was after she'd got us warmed up with arms stretch and the like, that the Sergeant suddenly turned to me and said: "Now, I want you to lead a crocodile, and everything you do, the rest has to follow."

There must have been a little bit of the devil in me that day. I looked at the girls. I knew most of them, I'd listened to their moans about going there, so I decided to side with the Sergeant for once; I'd give them something to moan about, so for the next ten minutes or so I led them in the wildest circle, something akin to a jungle-tribe having a jamboree. I did bunny jumps, top-turns, somersaults, and some movements they never knew existed. Anything I knew would have them gasping at the end of it. One by one they began to fall in strange heaps on the tennis court. Had a passing civilian noticed, they would have had the RAF up for cruelty. When I'd finished, the Sergeant herself was hard put to keep a straight face, and I pretended not to notice anything. I fully expected some retaliation back at the hut, but they were all too exhausted. I got some fine new titles that day though.

In a way we behaved at times like a slightly older version of the St. Trinian's girls, and one of the girls suddenly began a fad by sleeping in the nude. She'd read it was much healthier. Immediately we all followed her example, we all wanted to be in on the health lark. A couple of nights later another girl and I crept in the dark to the outside of the windows, after everyone seemed settled. We started a tap-tap-tapping on the windows so that in the end some of them had to get up. On another occasion we stood outside flapping sheets in front of the windows to scare them. There were plenty that would do anything, just to create some fun. These are memories thousands of us must live with, will never forget, but there was much sadness too, we discovered, to be remembered.

The girl-happy singing, of songs such as, "I'm gonna buy a paper doll . . . " when we'd stand in a row holding a row of paper dolls apiece, ones we'd torn to pass the time, could be abruptly shattered now and then. There were tears as well as laughter.

CHAPTER
FIVE

Sadness Strikes

Emotions could run high or very low of course, as they do with the late teens and early twenties. This was particularly so in the matter of love, and every now and then we witnessed misery without being able to help to alleviate it.

One morning, the pretty, fair-haired girl of a more serious disposition, in the bed next to mine, opened a letter. Someone from admin I think always delivered mail to the huts. After reading it her face was screwed strangely. My curiosity at her expression was just what she required at that moment. Betty turned, knowing she had a listener for her trouble. "It's from Mel. He was the Canadian I used to know. Well . . ." She heaved a deep breath as if someone one had just given her a blow, "I thought he must be dead or something."

I hadn't actually known about her big love for the Canadian aircrew fellow, but what I did know was that only three days previously she had been married to a slim fair-haired man on camp, who gave me the impression he looked too old for her.

She had been head-over-heels in love with Mel apparently, but after he'd been repatriated somewhere she hadn't heard from him for a full year and had no address. She'd accepted the natural events of the times we were having, either he'd decided to forget her or, typical of the young, had not thought to have her informed should he be killed. However, out of the blue had come the most beautiful love-letter, just three days too late. I forecast doom for her marriage as I saw the sheer misery in her eyes. And soon mine filled with it too as I tried to say something, but nothing seemed suitable.

It was morning too when a tall brunette hurried head-bent the full length of the hut, all eyes watching her, and again we seemed unable to tell her our sympathy in the fullness of words. The whisper had gone around that she'd just learnt that her fairly new aircrew husband had bought it during the night. His crew had failed to make it back to base.

My own turn came too. This time it was a love affair of a different sort, and he was dead too. My father, I knew, had become rather ill, and on my last leave I'd visited him in hospital. Here the doctor had sat mother and me down and said nothing further could be done. He was just fifty-four.

Despite knowing that I would eventually get the bad message, when the admin-Sergeant came shouting my name down the hut, saying almost brightly: "Telegram for you!" My knees turned to jelly. My instinct warned me what the form would say. Then I broke down after my shaking hands tore the envelope open. The message said simply: "Father dead — come home."

Without telephones, telegrams often heralded bad news. Of course as far as the Sergeant knew, it could have been a boyfriend wiring that he was coming to visit me. In my case fortunately, the girls didn't have time, before I began to cry, to suggest: "Oh, a DWE, smashing!" They would have been embarrassed and shattered at their mistake. A DWE was short for a "dirty weekend".

Unfortunately however, when I went across to tell my duty Sergeant, RAF type, that I'd like some compassionate leave, he grinned and said what the girls did not have time to. Tears tumbled again as I croaked: "No, my father's dead." The poor man didn't know which way to look.

I was unable to catch a train until morning. Trains were badly curtailed in those days, so I spent the most miserable night and then long journey, trying to contain my grief. On top of that an older type of fellow was chatting me up for the entire journey and tried to date me, which in my state felt loathsome, but I knew if I tried to tell anyone in the carriage why I was there that I would cry again. When I did reach home my mother, unfeelingly it seemed, said: "Why didn't you come home last night?"

Of course to go home for my father's funeral I got a genuine pass, but this reminds me of how we in signals became forgers. We were only allowed so many passes, but we had thought up a way of getting the official stamp on to the pass. We would tip the rubber stamp of our department sideways, so that the word "signals" was lost. This made it look just like the correct one.

Two or three of us would stand around excitedly while someone did it: "No, a bit further left," we might shout. We abandoned rules just to make life brighter really. Which of us doesn't?

We either took a train, or hitch-hiked out of sheer poverty. Being just the ranks we had to travel third class. Once though, Ricky (so-called because she was married to Dick) along with a friend, jumped into a first class, simply because there just wasn't room elsewhere. Only a naval officer occupied it. In casual conversation to her companion, Ricky said: "Mm, that ashtray would look nice in our hut. You'd think they'd provide us with ashtrays." She was busy using one. Whereupon the officer asked pointedly: "Would you really like it?"

No sooner had she grinned back when he took a penknife from a pocket and removed the said article, offering also to supply them with a mirror, which he began to try and dismantle, but fortunately it wouldn't budge. Ricky said: "We were astonished. We felt as if we had to accept, him being an officer and all that." On getting off the train, the ticket collector had seen them leave the first class carriage. He tackled them about the matter to which Ricky replied, "Yes, we came first class, and you'll never believe what we've got in our kit bags! Then the two of us ran like hell!" Because I knew her so well, I knew she was telling the truth when she said, "You know, it would never have occurred to me to pinch anything from a train like that." A case of dishonest camaraderie between uniforms, the officer must have thought, and obviously enjoyed it.

One weekend I managed the fare for a train to Lincoln where I was to meet Jennie. We'd agreed to go from there to Leeds where I had a cousin that we intended visiting. From there we thought we'd hitch a lift. We were walking along wondering if we'd have any luck when two soldiers, each on a motorbike stopped beside us.

"Where're you going girls?"

"Leeds," we shouted eagerly.

"Hop on," they invited, with almost naughty grins.

We hopped on nimbly and gratefully. The two tore off as if trying to escape an enemy. I'd recognised the bikes as being army despatch riders' and they despatched us at such speed we could barely breathe, as the gusts struck across our faces. I worried about Jennie who was slighter built than me as I saw her desperately trying to connect her left foot onto something solid. I prayed she wouldn't let slip with her arm from her driver's waist. The people we passed must have been left gaping, telling one another it shouldn't be allowed. We did the nearest thing to flying I've ever known, and in fact felt we did so going around corners. I clung with every muscle I knew to my own driver.

When they at last pulled to a halt, I truly felt my legs wobble as I got off the monster of a machine. Jennie's face seemed to give a silent sigh as I looked at her. We were quite aware that they expected us to floor them with our tongues about the devilish play they'd used us for. Instead we stood calmly and thanked them. They hadn't reckoned on picking up the two most complete madcaps ever let loose into service life! We left them speechless with surprise as we calmly turned and walked away. In truth it had been an absolutely hair-raising experience as they delivered us seventy miles in minutes in which our lives flashed before us. I know the soldiers must have often recounted the tale when they appeared pussy-struck at two slim WAAFs who seemed not to turn a hair at something which would have frightened the life out of even the men. It was the sort of crazy trick done by RAF pilots occasionally when with sheer joy at returning home, they would swoop low over an unsuspecting civilian.

Returning from Leeds another time with Valerie, it was getting rather late and we wondered if we'd make camp in time for midnight. If not, it would probably mean a charge for us. A stately Ford stopped and a very business-like man in a dark overcoat offered us a lift. He took off at a slow pace then casually asked where we were going and what time we had to be back. It must have been summer because it was about 10 o'clock and there was still some light. As soon as he realised there was a deadline for our passes, he seemed to worry much more than we had. He swept the little black car through country roads at an amazing speed. It was typical of the quite delightful way people seemed ready to put themselves out for someone in uniform.

On another return trip from Leeds, Valerie and I were being taken back to our lodging by private car. Two civilian men at a dance, I think the Star and Garter, had offered us the lift, and since we'd spent a pleasant evening with them, we accepted. They seemed rather older than the usual age we got involved with, and they expected no return for the evening's pleasure.

However, we did sit talking a while in the car. They were very interested in our life in the service, enough to make me wonder later if they were they writers or perhaps spies? Of course there was no way a good Britisher then would reveal anything. Anyway our very important signals were always in a five-letter code, and we had to despatch them without any loss of time. We wouldn't have found time to break even one line of code. Indeed one of my section was court-martialled for failing to do so once, and had actually tried to get me to lie to cover her failure, which, sensibly, I refused to do.

Anyway, as I sat in the front seat talking to my companion, I recognised a strong Jewish countenance. Then he confided to me one of the smaller secrets of the war. He told me very quietly, almost whispered, "By the way I am a Jew, but, for obvious reasons, I have changed my name to Brown." The reason he told me was probably because, when I had introduced myself, he would recognise my name as Jewish too, and probably thought I was a practitioner of the faith.

The amazing thing is I had no idea people, or rather Jews, in our island were so afraid that they found it vital to become plain British Brown. I had been, and still was, completely ignorant of the history of the Jews in Europe between the wars, and there was I, boldly using my name, not realising that, had Hitler reached our shores, I could well have been one for the ovens.

I held on to my ignorance not knowing what he meant, but friend Brown must have misinterpreted my silence, for before I left the car, he just sort of squeezed my hand, in a way which said there was some sort of bond between us. I fancied he was proud of my war effort. How miserably young and innocent I was. I never saw him again, but it was one of the rare odd moments in England which gave me a reminder — you are at war! His words had struck something terribly sinister into me.

Another such moment was when I watched about a thousand bombers overhead blacking out a summer sky. I knew our fighters would likely be forming the umbrella for them some thousands of feet higher. That was a moment I felt very proud to be one of the Lambs in Blue. Yet a visit to Jennie shortly after made me realise how much prouder she might feel.

CHAPTER
SIX

Visiting

I was expecting Jennie down from Lincolnshire one weekend, but I'd caught a cold somehow. Not wishing to disappoint her, I didn't report sick, thinking I could stick it out. My cold got much worse though, so that on the minute of her arrival in my hut on the Saturday, she could only stand and watch as I was being helped to sick-bay by an orderly. I could barely lift my hand to greet her astonishment, and later when the sick-bay officer looked into my throat he immediately suspected me of having diphtheria. I was rushed to an isolation hospital at once.

Dorothy, a lovely Scots lass in my hut, who once proudly told us she had never been christened, kindly brought Jennie to visit me, but I could only mouth words rather stupidly through the window from my bed. It was a wasted journey for them, but I was glad to learn Dorothy had entertained Jennie for the weekend.

About two days after I was returned to camp, a RAF bod spoke to me as I was waiting for a bus to Nottingham. He commented too on how pale I looked.

"I've just come out of hospital," I informed him, and to my surprise he said,

"So *you're* the one who got everyone confined to camp until the scare was over." Then he laughed, a little reluctantly I thought. My diphtheria turned out negative.

I, who had been cursing being stuck alone in hospital missing the lovely summer sun, hadn't known the whole camp had been kept in too. Of course a diphtheria outbreak was the last thing the authorities could chance with a war going on.

I returned Jennie's visit as soon as I felt better, and decided to go in civvies. I discovered her environment was rather different from mine. I alighted from a bus on a country road and walked a fair distance onto what turned out to be an airfield. The impression was of a vast empty space, very flat of course, and I saw that I was walking along the edge of a runway strewn with loose small stone chippings as if somebody ought to sweep it.

She had been watching for me and ran to meet me. Walking to her hut I was stopped and introduced to a RAF pilot she knew. It was the only one I managed to meet. The glamour I'd expected to see on an operational base was sadly missing for me. I saw no planes and when I commented to Jennie on this she took me towards a small hut, but would only let me poke my head into it. It was the RT hut and she barely let me have any time there, simply because we weren't supposed to be there. But those few minutes made up for what I'd expected to see. I can still hear now the voices of young men, voices without bodies — cursing and slashing their venom about the air as they fought battles in the sky. Their language understandably was not the sort they would have let their mothers hear, but I was well able to accept that in their position I would have voiced similar curses. Then surprisingly, German voices came down to us. Of course the airfield was empty! The courageous young men were somewhere above, somewhere we often think that heaven is. In actual fact, to them it was sometimes the nearest experience to hell. Jennie had to tear me away, "Come on, we'll get shot if we're caught."

Yet, despite the apparent emptiness, I experienced a thrill knowing it was where it all happened. I had met plenty of aircrew living it up off duty in Nottingham, and we'd built our own picture of them. We'd learnt how many put their faith in tokens of luck, perhaps a special silk scarf from their girlfriend, or even her knickers. It was very clear that most of them lived for the minute, took everything they could from life. It was, happily for them, wine, women and song, off duty, and the girls in blue never grudged them one bit of it, for we all knew that tomorrow they could surely die, or even that very night.

It was difficult to visualise how hard their lot was on duty. I have since learnt they even had no better huts than most. They suffered much lost sleep, endured cancelled orders, or worse, postponed ones which entailed nerve-breaking silences while they waited for new ones. They ate "wakey-wakey" pills on, and sometimes off, duty, and many got ulcers into the bargain, though their off-duty booze-ups might have helped too, for alcohol poured over nervous acidity is no help. Those who survived discovered them later.

It was over that very airfield, I was to learn shortly afterwards, that our friend Phil was blown to pieces one night when the Gerries had followed them in. Phil had been someone we'd danced with many times as one of our teenage crowd at home. Jennie took it as a great misfortune to go and talk to his parents later.

As Jennie recalls: "We worked safely underground while they counted their missions with the seriousness a doctor counts out tablets. We didn't see much of what was going on underground. Ours was just paperwork. No wonder they took all the fun they could lay their hands on. We never really understood the depth of their sickened emotions. Perhaps a control tower WAAF caught some of the terror which went on."

Certainly there were WAAFs who did see their misery. They were the ones who would accompany mangled, burnt and bleeding bodies in an ambulance, sometimes actually helping to pull them from a plane. One ex-WAAF told me: "I suffered a complete nervous breakdown afterwards. Imagine what they must have suffered."

The crews became a sort of family in the minds of the personnel who worked on ops bases. As Jennie remembers: "We sometimes used to stand and wait and really pray when the planes with such names as 'A for Able' or 'C for Charlie' hadn't turned up on time. Then there'd be great relief when we saw them come straggling back, no matter how late. We were all filled with happiness then."

Jennie took me to her hut. It was a corrugated iron one and it was fortunate it was summer, for in winter the snow easily, and rather prettily, curled into the parts where the corrugated sheets failed to meet. She also put on civvies and we went into Grantham.

Next day we went walking, and it's strange that though a war was on I remember the beauty of the fields. We came to a narrow river beside which was the most delightful cottage I'd ever seen. There was such peace, such silence as we strolled across seemingly endless miles of beautiful green, with golden sunshine enhancing it all. Young though I was, it made me feel, "This surely is what we're all trying to preserve".

A RAF bod in our section invited Valerie and me to his home for breakfast after arranging to give us a lift. He was to visit his wife who had a hairdresser's shop in Leeds. These were the sort of visits we began to enjoy for there was usually a nice meal too, though I did wonder sometimes where they got so much food.

This time it was apparent his wife had been expecting us when she seated us in their dining room. We each got a plate of food to surprise the Gods themselves. Our plates were artistically heaped with a pile of bacon, eggs, sausages, two chops, tomatoes, mushrooms and chips. The husband must have told his wife we'd come straight off night shift and would be starving, I'm sure. We could not believe our eyes and ate like starving tramps. No wonder the fellow made regular trips home!

Another memory of food for the Gods was when Jennie and I arranged to spend a leave in Edinburgh for a change. Sheila Duncan, a refined Scots girl who often sat doing tapestry in our hut, had suggested an address we could stay at. We came to look upon our hostess as Aunt Minnie.

One night she took us to a centre where we learned for the first time the wonderful excitement of Scottish reels and the immense energy of Scottish people. That evening we were introduced to various people and it must have been my name again that got us invited to a Jewish home. The two sons had been kind enough to take us into the dancing while the elders played whist in the next room, and at the end they invited us to take supper with them.

It was their Sabbath, and the whole family seemed to be there and they seemed thrilled to be entertaining two girls who were away from home in the cause of war. They emphatically told us that.

Highly polished silver graced beautiful linen as we tucked into plates of the most delightful food, which we'd almost forgotten existed. We tried not to eat like tramps. The only blot on that evening for me was that we'd already accepted the supper invitation when a young Scotsman in full dress of kilt with all its fascinating accessories asked to escort me home.

Jennie and I had both fallen in love with him instantly on seeing him framed in the doorway as he joined the evening's occasion. It almost broke my heart to tell him, "I'm sorry, but I've already made an arrangement", and went on to tell him where we were going. Perhaps I'd been reading the *People's Friend* too much, and I was already in love with every man in a kilt. I spent days sighing over the thought of what might have been.

It wasn't just the food we liked of course if we visited a home. We'd got so used to living in huts, that just to enter a house was becoming an alien feeling to us. However I got lucky in that respect. One night at the Nottingham Palais I was invited to dance by a tall, handsome soldier who had the squarest chin I've ever seen. At the end of the night his sister invited me home for tea, along with Valerie who'd danced with his friend, but I felt sure he had been the initiator of the idea.

The pleasant house on the outskirts of the city became like a home to us, and it was good to smell home-baking again. Some families were extremely kind in realising how much we did miss home.

I became very involved with the family, and it was during an outing on bicycles that his sister, Evelyn, and I both fell headlong into a deep ditch one night. The blackout was always a problem for everybody, so that riding cycles was almost lunacy. We'd missed a corner.

Another cycle ride with Eric, the brother, put me for the first time on police files. He'd invited me to his camp dance, and the only way to get there after bussing so far was to walk or ride, as we did. The trouble was, cycles were in short supply, so I sat on the crossbar while Eric steered. These cycles were kept in a specific spot for the soldiers' use.

It was hard to believe, but a West Yorkshire policeman spotted us on a country road where there was nothing for miles but cows. He must have been desperate for a case of any sort. He charged us with riding "two on a bike".

Eric, with chivalry, tried to take the blame, but "Stubborn" refused to lose an opportunity. Back at camp I was requested to visit the commanding officer; "What's this you've been up to Barnett?" But she had all the crime details before her. She sort of smiled and said: "Don't do it again. I'll just write a letter pleading guilty. OK?"

"Thank you," I murmured sheepishly. I got fined ten shillings.

The war struck me with horror when one day Eric asked me to accompany him to visit a friend's parents. He was short of bravado and needed some moral support. They'd just learned of the death of their younger son at sea. This followed close on the heels of the death of their other son a few months previously. Now they had none. Eric warned: "Their mother turned white overnight. I'm dreading going."

We entered an immaculately kept home. She walked us around a beautifully laid out garden, which was rich with flowers. Indoors again, she pointed out a photograph saying: "These are my two sons." I can't remember anything after that. Her words were drifting into my thoughts, getting themselves lost.

We walked back to Eric's home, too numbed for words. There had been such an unnatural calm about the white-haired woman. She showed no sign of disturbed emotions in her welcome. We were the ones who had felt ill at ease. She'd seemed surrounded by a spiritual calm.

On my next leave I heard of the similar death of one of my own friends in the navy. It was strange, but things always seemed to have a blacker look when I heard about deaths within the walls of houses. I suppose it was the fact that people in houses were always so much older and took death so much more seriously.

In camp we were all young, all living life to the full, all bent on living forever. Yet some older folk must have had a tough sense of survival too. I remember Eric's mother saying to me one day: "I cannot understand why they don't send our boys over there. They're the finest bunch anywhere." She was referring to the Sherwood Foresters, and she was right about that. They seemed a splendidly built bunch who could take on anyone. It seemed almost as if the army was holding them back for something special.

In the meantime, Eric had fallen in love with me, though not I with him, but he persisted enough to make me think I might be. He asked that we should become engaged. I capitulated, just before he went off to "somewhere in England" — but I continued to have fun.

We often made our own entertainment in camp. Evelyn Taylor from Manchester had been on the stage. She would line us up and teach us the professional way to dance as a chorus. I remember singing a duet while we did impressive actions to the song "White Christmas".

Occasionally we were treated to an ENSA concert on camp when we had to endure many blue jokes for the sake of the men, some of which we could not understand, but the men guffawed.

Evelyn and I also found an open-air swimming-pool where we took great risks as we invented crazy new kinds of double-dives and suchlike.

On another occasion she persuaded me to let her transform me in aid of a fancy dress dance on camp. She no longer had theatrical make-up of course, so to make me into the character "Topsy", she simply smoothed a film of black shoe-polish — and there was plenty of that on camp — onto me. Then she tied my hair in rags and found me the weirdest assortment of garments. I came up such a magnificent Topsy, that Eric didn't even begin to recognise me. He'd managed to get away and join me for that special night. I teased him for half an hour before he recognised me. He had stayed as a soldier.

I had to spend a long time later on, in the cold early morning, trying to scrub myself clean with water which was just tepid, but we'd had such a good night I did not complain about that to Evelyn. It also made up for it when Eric's family told me they'd heard all about it, and Eric himself said: "If I'd had a camera, I'd have put that photograph in a golden frame!"

We held a sports day too at Watnall — which was where HQ was, and our signals team won the girls' relay race. My name had been put forward by someone who had seen me running for a bus one day and thought I'd be an asset to the team. It must have been the first time ever that a runner was chosen that way. I took the final sprint position, but it was just as I reached the tape that

I gasped as a pulled hamstring caught me. I managed to collect my prize though, which was a large pack of talcum.

On that day too, we all got an extra special treat. A fresh strawberries and cream stall was set up, and they had allowed visitors into the field. My mother had managed to come down for a week to stay with Eric's family and she and his mother had come along for the occasion, as well as Eric. I'm sure we all felt at the end that it had been a very satisfying, most enjoyable day, the sort the English can really enjoy.

I was asked to do the "met" reports now and then. I neither knew from whence the report was channelled into my earphones, nor where it went on my repeating it down a tube. We were so conditioned to not repeating what we knew, saw, or heard, it reached the stage where we thought we must not ask questions either. I still don't know who got the reports. Perhaps it went to the pilots in the air. I had only had it emphasised to take great care in making sure I said the words "nine" and "five" so that they would not be confused. Another WAAF explained how to do it.

I was on duty one night and I'd just finished reading such a report when I heard some special news on the grapevine, which was to alter the whole course of my life in a sense. As war news seldom filtered through to us, we knew the whispers meant it was something really big.

The news, which had transgressed the normally observed silence of movements, was that "D-day" had arrived. It was the start of "Operation Overlord", the invasion of Europe that they had been holding back so much of our fighting force for; an operation that would soon take Eric to France. I knew Eric's mother would be clapping her hands, glad that some really super boys were going across to settle it.

CHAPTER
SEVEN

Passion Without Guilt

The mad activity on the south coast had come and gone, though it is something which may never be forgotten, and somewhere among the many thousands Eric went across to France.

In a sense I felt I was still being watched because of him, but in a nice sense only.

Eric's brother-in-law was a Sergeant-Policeman at our camp too, and I was often bumping into him. A striking memory of Dennis is that he was so cold sometimes as he did "road duty", watching to see no unofficial persons entered camp, he would stand taking sips from a small bottle of brandy, which he kept hidden in his outer coat pocket.

He would hand me a sip too when I passed him in the cold black nights to go on duty. It seemed very cheering when there was snow or frost about, but I seemed to cause much concern when I laughingly mentioned this to Eric's mother who immediately looked as if I'd started her thinking that her daughter was married to an alcoholic. She made no comment on my sips, and I only thought Dennis needed the brandy.

He hadn't a particle of fat for warmth though he was tall.

Girls will be girls, I was discovering, just as boys will be boys, and that included myself. Eric's going to France, which it took us a little while to discover, began to cement further the idea that I was not ready to marry him — or perhaps it was just that I was not ready for marriage at all. I was still too young. He was five years my senior.

However, I left things as they were, but joined in the fun as usual with the rest of the girls. I soon met Eldon, a Canadian aircrew man and felt only slightly guilty as I found myself enjoying his company along with others of his station. After about three months when we'd enjoyed dances, the theatre, and joining his friends for drinks, he let out the news that he was married — not an unusual situation of those times.

Eldon's great joy about England was the theatre. I took him to a show one week, which happened to have one of the bluest comedians in the business. He guffawed his usual fair face into a screwed red mask of enjoyment, and would tell me that such smutty stuff would never be allowed back home. He was all for the English about enjoying it, and though I didn't particularly thrill to it myself, I was always delighted he found such enjoyment. I was, of course, aware it might have been his last good laugh, despite the St. Christopher medal I'd bought him, supposed to bring luck to travellers. Perhaps there's laughter in heaven.

Like most people, we girls often confided in one another, and this was how I learnt some strange tales of

61

passion among the WAAFs. Ross, as I mentioned, was rather a naughty type, particularly as she was also married. She met an aircrew bod of the Australian Force, a dark magnetic type called "Lucky", and she let herself go overboard about him. She had almost no scruples, which was her business, but she should not have got Valerie into a fix one night . . .

Ross had arranged for them and two Australians to take one of those breaks which prompted the song, "I never said thanks for that lovely weekend". Valerie however, was pure innocence then, and thought because two rooms had been booked, she and Ross would be sharing, yet she inexplicably found herself in an hotel room with Lucky's friend. She was quite upset about it later as she told me, and was thereafter much more cautious about Ross's ideas for having a good time. Valerie looked as pure as she was too, and far too sweet to create a fuss.

Ross got both Valerie and me involved one afternoon, but it turned to our advantage. She wanted to see Lucky and took us with her to the hotel she knew he'd be at. However, as so often happened with aircrew, he'd been summoned to fly. Ross's idea that Lucky would buy us all tea flopped until she spied one of his friends. She went to work with such charm we still got our delicious afternoon tea in the most expensive hotel in town, which none of us could afford.

Blind dates seemed to happen a lot, and it was one that Valerie arranged for me, which left us howling with laughter. She had met a Londoner and I could see she was quite keen on him. He'd invited her to his London home and just happened to have a friend. Had Valerie a friend, he wanted to know? London. I'd always wanted to see London. I jumped at the chance, caring not what the friend could turn out to be — he could be ugly or arrogant or shy, I didn't really mind.

It was arranged that I'd stay at Peter's Wimbledon home, and Valerie at Harry's, and we'd all spend the two days together. First we went to a cinema to see Bing Crosby and I found Peter a most pleasant boy, and none of the things I've mentioned. He was in khaki, about six foot, very fair, with healthy cheeks and earnest blue eyes, and he told me his father was a high official in Wimbledon. They had a comfortable home, but, of course, I was just there for London, and to help Valerie with her infatuation.

Next day, Sunday, was a clear fresh day so it was agreed we'd take a boat onto the Thames. We'd already been for a long walk that took us over Wimbledon Common in the morning, after which we'd called into a pub where Valerie and I drank shandies and the boys, beer. I was quite looking forward to just sitting getting a good view of London via the river.

The boat trip though turned out to be more of a commando course with the boys in their berets. They rowed well, and manoeuvred us to a delightful spot where gracious trees of drooping leafy boughs shaded us perfectly. I knew as soon as I saw the shaded area that sightseeing, the little we had done, was finished.

It was Peter rather than Harry who developed a sudden attack of passion. So much so we had great luck that the boat did not turn turtle completely. I

63

remember gripping with panic the low bulwarks as the heavy wooden structure rocked and rolled to within an inch of old father Thames, while one of his London sons flung kisses as if he'd just learned what fun it all was. We all resurfaced, cheeks aglow, and suddenly became stumped for conversation. I realised moderate Peter had a great reserve of energy, which it was wrong for him to hold back too long. Valerie and I laughed for days afterwards, and somehow she'd already gone off Harry though she never said why.

Love and passion regularly flared and died like rockets, I discovered, during the war. There was little of the quiet advance that home love affairs had been. It seemed obvious that men had a terrible fear of dying before they'd experienced every bit of living, and between eighteen and twenty-five, living was loving.

One of the funniest tales I've been told was of one girl who decided on a DWE with a civilian, who was nevertheless working on engines for aircraft. Zena was the type who'd be all perfume, as well as frills on her weekends. She climbed up to their room, she said, when her escort told her he wouldn't be long. He'd wanted to discuss some sort of business with someone who was at the hotel.

She prepared and lay down waiting, but the minutes ticked by and kept on ticking until she was unable to stay awake any longer.

"The nerve of it," she said afterwards, "I've never been so insulted. Fancy putting business first. He didn't even apologise next morning. You wouldn't get anyone in uniform behaving like that."

We'd sometimes hear such a tale as we sat around the tall iron stove that had personality enough to appear to be listening too as it breathed out cokey hot fumes about us. And the most daring tale was of a beautiful WAAF with curly brown hair. Her aircrew lover decided it was getting too expensive — so many nights to pay for, so he hit on a plan. He booked a room in a boarding house for himself then smuggled his girl in to share it. Sometimes he was lucky and got a double bed too. The next morning when tea was brought round he would open the door quite innocently, take the tea, then remind the servant his young lady was to join him for breakfast which he asked to have put on his bill. While this conversation was going on, our heroine was curled up under the bed. She slipped out later, walked round the block then returned and rang the doorbell. Indeed, passion could be very expensive in those days and boarding-house keepers must have been the nouveau riche of the times. They must also have encountered some very beautiful love stories, many of which are still secretly wrapped away in memory only. A war dashes conformity against the wall particularly when youth takes the reins. I wonder what happened to all those love tokens once the peace bells tolled? In many cases they'd have to be flung out, and preserved only in the memory.

There were also WAAFs who became known as "Chop Girls", and this was nothing to do with food. They were so-called because they'd had a succession of boyfriends, each of whom had been killed on ops. There

65

were no tokens connected with them, only the nasty tag of, "Drop it, she's a chop girl".

The last I heard Lucky had stayed that way with Ross, and I presume returned to his homeland. Ross however, went on to have three husbands at the last count. She once told me, almost gaily, that she had no faith in either men or marriage, as if she'd been warned off it long before she grew to womanhood. I'd had no such warnings but came to realise that a lot of men, married or not, do pack their passions with everything else they take to war. No wonder my father was reluctant to let me go.

Valerie later met and married a soldier and my last knowledge was that everything was fine with them. Perhaps it was just as well I'd advised her when she asked what I thought: "No, you don't tell the man you want to marry that you've been to bed with someone. How can you know for sure he hasn't done the same?" I was thinking of that strong medicine, human kindness, which was often needed and often given to help "the twitch" that aircrew, in particular, lived with. Some of them could tell a girl about that more easily than telling another crewman. The twitch was something most of them got, felt ashamed of having, and could forget for a while in the arms of a girl.

Life seemed to have many turnings then, and I made one more when my mother asked if it was possible for me to get nearer home. Loneliness seemed to have struck her rather badly. I managed to get a posting north, though I felt sad at leaving my friends, and I took many nice memories with me on the train.

I still had my pageboy haircut, which three of us had changed to on impulse one day when we'd dived into a hairdresser's. I recalled the wonderful weekend at Ross's home, and going to see "The Desert Song" in Liverpool. I smiled inwardly about the two airmen who said to me: "There's a lad in our hut who's wild about you. He's an Honourable! You want to get yourself out with him." I couldn't understand in that case why he hadn't asked me. Perhaps, like me, he was shy of asking. Oh, so many memories. And the girl too, who'd borrowed my uniform to get married in because mine seemed smarter. Did her marriage succeed? I hope so. Then there was the girl whose blanket I was looking after — I don't know where she went — she had wanted me to meet her brother, but I never did. There are so many unfinished stories from Watnall, but I was on my way to meet a new crowd. Eric was still in France and I knew I would miss his family dreadfully despite my uncertain feelings for him. I had lovely companionship with his sisters, and had seen a great and admirable personality in his mother. His father, like most fathers, had never said much.

I'd learnt too that WAAFs could be as tough as any man could when, during a parade in Nottingham one blistering day, we'd been kept standing for an hour waiting for the hierarchy to appear, to keep our appointment. To my surprise, an airman in the line beside me fainted, and from then on they kept fainting all over the place. That parade did end up in the newsreels. The whole left side of the parade remained almost intact and wondering at the weakness of their male counterparts. We'd always been led to believe we were the weaker sex.

It was fortunate that we were strong because my toughness was to be tested in the months ahead, more than it had been at HQ.

WAAFs won awards too, and I remember one walking around our hut and showing us the oak-leaf she'd won. I knew it was for bravery for my father had won it too, and I gave her my warm admiration.

I'd seen up until then we were doing a good job, and as I recently reminded my cousin, who went into the WAAFs expecting to sew parachutes but ended up doing any odd job nobody else seemed around to do: "But you were just as important. Somebody had to do the odd jobs. It was lucky you had so many skills at your fingertips."

She'd been a seamstress, cook, clerk, and had in fact outstripped the normal cook's skill, it appeared, when all the bods had suggested she take over the job for good. Somebody had said of the regular one: "It's not surprising she's on the sick, she'll have us all on it if she turns up again."

One WAAF reminded me too, during research "They didn't pull their punches either when they put us on a charge. One night, I was five minutes late getting back. I got three days in the kitchen peeling spuds as well as being confined to camp for a week but it did teach me to watch the time after that.

Anyway it never stopped me smiling it seemed, for my signature tune from the other girls was 'You are my sunshine'. Believe me, there were times when I needed to hear it to cheer myself up."

CHAPTER
EIGHT

Back to the Cold North

Eric had said to me one day: "No wonder you never seem to feel the cold. It's damn cold up your area. You must be hardened to it."

He'd been up north on manoeuvres, and had thought it many degrees cooler, and now I was returning there.

I arrived at Kenton to be billeted in a redbrick house, one of many taken over to house forces' personnel. Summer was about ending, the house was draughty, and there was no heating and no hot water.

Getting up in the dark on winter mornings was the nearest to misery I remember though I'd begun to find fun with my new crowd. We would fling ourselves with cold curses into our uniform having attempted to warm shirt and underwear in the warmth of the bed we'd left. Then we'd cringe into the freezing darkness. It was sheer joy, one morning, when we reached the main road, to see a workmen's hut there. Standing before it was an open brazier of bright, red-hot cokes. Teeth chattering, we toddled up and requested, "Do you mind if we warm ourselves?" We were all menstruating at the time and therefore feeling the cold more that morning.

The two workmen took one look at us. "Come on, hinney, get yourselves warmed." They could hardly believe we were living without heating. It was not surprising that a few of us ended up with colds and diarrhoea that winter, and whoever got the second got dubbed with the title, "Queen of the Netty".

We walked into camp for breakfast and from there walked to the turnip field on top of the hill. We crossed both the turnips and the field and literally disappeared into a hole in the middle of it, just as a rabbit would and without a trace. The strange entrance led us into an underground operations block, which is still there to this day.

I'd begun to smoke at Watnall, which Eric hated, and at Kenton the habit hardened because everyone seemed to work with a tinlid full of cigarette ash by his or her machine. It was smart to smoke then.

I became friendly with three girls in particular, Ricky, Peggy and Nora, also in teleprinters, who lived in the area too.

Home was very dull, and I had seen my brother only once since I'd joined up. That was on a special occasion when I'd been invited to be bridesmaid at his wedding. He had joined the RAF too, also in signals. I missed the HQ crowd very much at first.

However, Ricky turned out to be good fun to be with and had a quick mind, which was full of jokes. At first we went ice-skating (as if we were not cold enough) though, being no experts, we were constantly in a sweat there. We met two Canadians at the rink one day who asked us to accompany them to Hexham, which they'd been told was an interesting place to see, and could we show them the route from Durham.

We agreed when we saw they had quite a nice black car for the journey, which caused us as much sweating though as our skating did. Somewhere along the route they pulled into a lay-by, the result being I had the greatest off-putting struggles of my girlhood days with the driver. Unlike Peter on the Thames who wanted only kisses, the Canadian thought he was onto a good thing. The result was, he said later: "My life! Are you all as strong as this?" when he'd failed in his desires.

Ricky, who'd had a less amorous companion beside her, nevertheless had to slide low down in the seat as she passed through her home village, where her husband's relatives lived. "It would have been just like the thing to be seen. And the trouble was the story would have been blown out of all proportion, knowing the village lot."

The little car survived the storm however, and they sportingly bought us a meal in Hexham, but Ricky and I have never forgotten the day we put our trust in two strangers, one of whom was a particularly likely lad.

We occasionally went for drinks with the GPO fellows who constantly worked beside us, and some of them pestered us too.

A silly memory is when we noticed peas in their pods growing on camp one day, Ricky and I went longingly and pinched a handful each. We both came from country villages and fresh peas were a reminder of better times. It was my first fresh raw vegetable for three years.

Ricky was one of a bunch of WAAFs once accused of mutiny. When at St. Helens sometime previously, she was in a crocodile under the stern eye of a WAAF admin-Sergeant who'd come from Prague. As they were marching, a great puddle loomed ahead, the leaders tried to pass it on the side. That though, was not in the book of WAAF rules. The Sergeant told them: "When you march with me, you go through a ★★★ puddle." They were never sure whether, because of her accent, which was heavily foreign, her penultimate word had been "damn" or "damp".

They refused to march through it on the argument they'd just cleaned their damn shoes anyway. An officer suddenly appeared and said they must obey orders. There was a right shindy when they were warned they would be charged with mutiny, so they marched through the thing. However the Sergeant never reappeared after that, so they felt victory was ultimately theirs, Ricky said.

The next day the same crocodile was followed through a farm track by a very noisy gander. Ricky said: "I was last and had a terrible feeling my rear was about to be attacked, but after the previous day's warning I didn't know whether to laugh or cry; never mind, we did manage to get safely through a gate before it got me." So discipline for WAAFs was as strict as in any men's army.

During the winter Peggy got a nasty cold. "I just feel like going to bed with it," she said rather miserably. Then she looked at me. "How about if I breathe germs all over you? Then we can have a week in sick-bay together. At least we'd be warm in there."

"Carry on," I answered, half in fun, so she leaned forward and did so. I really did get a beautiful cold too, and we actually spent a week in sick-bay. Then shortly after that we were all moved from our house into camp. If anything, that seemed even colder. We slept in concrete huts that showed no way in which heating of any sort could be fixed. At least the house had had a fireplace where we sometimes burnt rubbish. However, there was an abundance of hot water in the ablutions.

I shared a room with a fantastic blonde named Nora, who had just lost her husband, killed in the war. I never giggled so much as I did with Nora. We seemed to share the same ridiculous sense of humour at that time, and I'm sure it was something to do with the hardships we were suffering which sent us to extremes of incredulity with our lot. We had to make up for it in laughter.

We had cold stone floors and getting into bed seemed misery each night. One of us had to stay and switch off the light by the door before we settled down and we often managed to stub a toe on the only bits of furniture, the beds.

I had an idea. I searched about at home for some nails and a hammer, which I used to place the nails, so that by a length of string pulled across, I could then lie in bed and pull off the light. It worked beautifully, but

74

when we heard on the grapevine that an officer was inspecting, I took fright.

She was already at the door before I could pull down my invention. Her eyes fell like arrows straight on to it, and she stood gazing at it, eyebrows raised, for quite some seconds. Then I was astounded to hear her say: "What an ingenious idea." I nearly sunk to the floor with relief, knowing how little it took to get on a charge, depending on which senior it was. I had been visualising: "You are charged with damaging government property," in big red letters.

After that Nora and I would lie, sometimes for ages, making ridicule of life, and knowing I just needed to poke out a finger and thumb to switch off the light. The smallest things would entertain us then, and we had no "whose turn" arguments after that.

I remember enjoying playing netball at Kenton, something we had not got around to at HQ. One day an officer stood and watched the match and later sent for me, asking me where I'd played before. She sent my name off to be considered for the Air Force team I think, but I'd left England before I heard more of that — another lost opportunity. In the meantime I still felt rather bored at times, so it was a well-timed moment when Peggy and I spied a notice in camp, asking for volunteers to work in the local infirmary at off-duty times.

We presented ourselves at the RVI, and were vetted by matron herself who looked even sterner than some of our Sergeants, despite her frills. However, she seemed to think we were the right material, though only after she'd examined our fingernails. We were then instructed to go there whenever we could, and help in any way we were asked, in a certain ward.

From that moment life brightened up immensely, and Peggy and I went regularly to do our bit, and our suitably plague-free hands found satisfaction in helping with a number of light duties. But the great fun in going there was that we were put onto a ward, which was choc-a-bloc with our own wounded soldiers. Like any large bunch of young men, they were rather hilarious to be with despite their wounds and illnesses, though of course, some were in a state that would only allow them to lie and watch the fun. We were extremely pleased we'd volunteered, even if only to try and cheer the boys. In between we wound up bandages, made up and stripped beds, carried meals to the patients, and giggled forever until matron or doctors appeared. We even danced with the men who were capable of dancing, to a portable gramophone in the evenings. The highly polished ward floor made an excellent dance-floor, and the boys seemed pleased to see us. Peggy, a dark brunette, was a naturally happy person with the type of turned-up mouth that shows it.

One afternoon though, the boys really put the wind up me. There was silence in the ward, which was rather unusual. A small crowd of them was gathered round one bed, and I wondered if they were quietly discussing some gripe they had with the hospital, or whether a mate was getting much worse. As far as I could see they were getting great treatment, in fact being treated like heroes.

The bomb dropped however, when for some reason, I had to pass by the aforementioned bed. I was suddenly grabbed by two of them and plonked flat on the bed, too shocked almost even to scream, though in the end I did, as loudly as I dared in a hospital. I struggled like a wildcat, so more hands had to hold me, and then what they had planned took place. A tallish ginger Scots lad calmly took a pair of surgical scissors, and while I was held rigid with soldiers and wonder, for they'd appeared such a smashing bunch until then, he snipped one of the curls off my head. Then they released me with full apologies and I watched with surprise as he placed it into his pocket. All this time Peggy had been grinning from the other side of the ward.

I'd changed my hairstyle after coming north, to the Maria-cut, or bubble-cut as it was also called. Ingrid Bergman had started the new trend in the film "For Whom The Bell Tolls", and we were all hoping to look as good as she did.

The noise in the ward was largely overlooked because of the war circumstances which had caused it to be full of soldiers, but I now wonder what must have been the thoughts of the occupants of the ward opposite, who were in hearing distance across the corridor. I know they must have heard the carryings-on.

Across the corridor lay the captured and wounded Germans. I remember the first time I had occasion to visit them. I was busy giving out dinners that noon, when a plump soul, a Mrs Best, who dished up the meals in the kitchen, took it upon herself to be the adjudicator of nations. She filled one trayful of mugs with soup to the brim, and the next trayful only half-full of the broth which was really rich and delicious. She glanced at me: "There, take those ones in to those Gerries." After a further second, she said, "Our lads deserve the best." She was pointing to the half-filled mugs.

I carried the laden tray across the corridor, hoping not to spill any down my crepe-silk dress, as I was feeling very ponderous as to whether or not I should speak at all. I was so used to larking about with our British boys, but these were the enemy. I'd never set eyes on the enemy before, or any German in fact. It was a very strange feeling as I entered the ward, but I think Mrs Best's words had already instilled a feeling of rejection into me.

I entered to find a full ward of young, mostly very fair-haired and rather good-looking boys. They seemed no older than I. It looked as though they were hardly daring to breathe even. They were mostly sitting upright, all very neat and tidy in their pyjamas, like a bunch of children who'd been warned: "Now don't dare move and spoil those beds." Although the ward was full, it was like moving through a graveyard.

I walked silently from one bed to the next, carefully placing a mug on each locker as I went. Each man in turn stared at me, nodded slightly, and some, in the quietest of voices, said something which I took to mean: "Thank you." Each voice was so low, subjugated in the presence of their enemy, that it was as if they were living in the throes of acute fear. And in my youthful imaginative way, I wondered if they thought I, a young and attractive enough woman, had been specially sent in to bleed them of secrets. I felt like some sort of dressed-up Mata Hari as I glanced at the very serious faces full of some sort of worry.

There was neither movement nor sound of voice even after I was well clear of the ward, I'm sure. I really wondered if they'd get one of them to taste the soup first before all venturing to drink it. It was a vivid example of circumstantial behaviour.

It was the last time I saw the Germans, and therefore had no need to ponder about them again, because I now made another life-turn. Despite feeling more fulfilled with the hospital work, there was still something disturbing me. I feel sure it was something to do with my engagement. I could neither accept nor reject it, or perhaps I was too soft-hearted to break an engagement to a soldier who was already suffering, I thought, in France.

Eric had been back to England once and had also managed to visit me. Luckily, he'd picked one of the days I had gone home. Because of boredom I'd started to help my mother with some special cleaning. She'd wanted some boxes of books and photographs packed away in the loft, so I agreed to climb up and do it. I'd put on an overall and wrapped my hair in a scarf because of the usual muck one finds in lofts. Then just as I'd finished the job and stepped off the ladder, the doorknocker slammed rather urgently so I ran to answer it. I was amazed to find Eric standing on the steps in full despatch rider's gear, goggles, gauntlets, the lot.

He got such a surprise at my appearance, it took him some seconds to tell me: "I'm on my way to Scotland. They don't know I'm here, so I haven't got long." Then he'd laughed heartily when he understood why my nose and hands, and most other parts of me, were so grimy. It was the last time that I was to see my fiancé, as such. It had been such a rushed visit I'd forgotten to tell him I'd applied, or at least answered a call, for volunteer personnel to go to France. The unexpectedness and rush of the visit had knocked things of importance from my mind, though I did remember to tell him I'd just finished a fortnight's course for engaged WAAFs in the art of domestic achievement. Ricky, being newly married was persuaded to do it too.

The Air Force or someone had rightly realised that none of us were getting any sort of training for marriage in the domestic sense. We were relieved of normal duties to learn cooking, entertaining and general household duties. It was a very useful course, for which they'd fully furnished one of the redbrick houses. It was a stupendous opportunity in that we not only cooked some delicious dishes, but we also sat and ate them with officers as guests. Jennie happened to come home on weekend leave at the time and I was able to invite her as a guest also.

It was just before I started the course that the request for people for France went up on the notice board. I desperately wondered if Jennie had had the same request at her camp. It was natural instinct between us to know she would volunteer too if given the chance. We both had a sort of primitive sense of adventure for anything, particularly if it sounded insane.

To make sure, I disobeyed orders for the first time and used the teleprinter system for my own benefit. By sheer luck Jennie was on duty, and I just managed to get her reply: "Yes, I've volunteered," before our conversation was curtly snapped off with a warning. I was lucky not to be charged.

Of course I hadn't known immediately that I would be accepted to go, and in fact the commanding officer had a serious talk with me. She warned me: "You realise of course, that it could be very tough. You might not even have a bed to sleep in, and you'll probably have to wash in freezing water out of a pail." Her graphic words made no difference. I still wanted to go.

She gave me a thoughtful look before saying: "You will probably hear something shortly." I hadn't explained that Eric was in France, my love affair in question.

In a few weeks I was given a final leave, and at the same time issued with a booklet on everyday French phrases which would be useful and I eagerly began to brush up the language. Jennie came on leave at the same time and I cannot really say what thoughts were predominant in my mind for that week. Our parents seemed unduly worried that we were to go abroad at all; but I do recall that the week dragged by.

It was already December, and bitterly cold as I said goodbye to my friends and the boys at the hospital. I'd been given my jabs, and foolish as ever, had ignored the warning not to go drinking at all. But the GPO men had wanted to give me a farewell drink along with some of the girls, and I hated refusing, but it made me sick. It was not the "Nut Brown Ale" I'd requested. I only had one, but probably the inoculations combined with it. Some of the WAAFs I've shared memories with, have told me they managed to get drunk, but in every case, only once. They hadn't enjoyed it. My turn to get drunk had not yet arrived then.

My Godmother took me into town and suggested a gift to me. She wanted to buy me a beautiful package of some special face powder. I graciously accepted, remembering not to drop secrets about where I thought we were heading. My officer's warning made it seem unlikely that face powder would be of much use to me, and apart from that I never used the clogging stuff. And of course I did not want to worry my mother about the stark nature of events I was about to endure. I simply said I was posted abroad.

I left my mother sad-faced at the prospect of another Christmas without any family, and it was with a kind of sober meditation that Jennie and I travelled westwards to West Kirby. It seemed a funny direction for France, but fake trails, as well as fake rumours, were expected in those days.

In fact I only learnt on my research that Jennie had not a scrap of an idea where she was supposed to be going. She'd simply volunteered to go abroad "somewhere". And of course not even the best of friends ever discussed war movements of any sort. If we'd both been told we were about to leave for the moon, which was a crackpot-dream in the forties, we'd still, I'm sure, have adhered to the poster warning: "Remember, Walls have Ears!"

CHAPTER
NINE

Leaving England's Shore

We arrived at West Kirby with kit bags stuffed to bursting point. Kenton had been cold, but West Kirby was reminiscent of the ice age. I have an agonising memory of bathing under showers in a cold hangar-like building, through which blew an Arctic gale, adding to the horror of cold water on our soft female bodies. I picture now having to wait around in there one morning in our uniforms when someone pointed out Sarah Churchill. It struck me how even the aristocracy went blue just like the rest of us as I glanced at her pale narrow face which had a veil of blue ageing her cheeks. She was bluer than most.

On top of the cold, we were stuck in camp, with the limit of pleasure becoming a walk around the camp perimeter. The secrecy network took no chances. Parades helped to relieve the boredom. One morning we were gathered en masse and with the usual command: "Eyes Right!" We adjusted our formation. Having got ourselves perfect they then commanded us to "Stand at ease!"

We waited shiftily for some minutes and then were brought to full awareness again by a further command: "ATTEN-TION!" There was no secrecy about this sort of performance. We knew someone with rings on their sleeves was about to give us the once-over. I'd been a member of the WAAFs for over three years, and it seemed a long time since I'd been inspected on parade, especially the sort where we got looked over as if she were looking at fish on a slab. So I was relieved to recall that I'd pinned up my hair carefully into a neat roll, well off my collar, as I watched the slow gait of a high-ranking officer (and it's clever how we learnt to do that without turning our heads) accompanied by a worse-looking Flight Sergeant.

My smugness was shattered as they reached me, and I was ordered to stand at ease. It's a nasty feeling when there are hundreds of others around you. Was something hanging down? Or had a button's thread deliberately chewed through itself at the crucial moment? No, that was impossible. They'd sewed them on as if they would have us forever. My stomach heaved when I was asked for my name and number.

"Oh you dratted number!" I thought, "You're for it now." Yet I really could not imagine what I'd forgotten. Then the Flight Sergeant ordered me to report to a certain hut at 2pm sharp, after writing my identification in her notebook. Then she said: "As you were!" I stood to attention, far from what I'd started the parade as though. I'd turned from stiff to limp.

I reported on the dot of two, neater than ever I hoped. Inside the hut I was lined up with five others in front of a counter. We were each handed some items of tropical kit — topee and bush jacket to be precise — then told to begin trying them on. Past the end of the counter we met the photographer, a tall man who was rolling some sort of newsreel camera. My ghastly fears, along with those of the others, suddenly turned to rather relieved giggles as we vainly tried to produce some glamour in the unnatural headgear. I thought: "What with French booklets and now tropical kit, where on earth are we off to?" I still refrained from telling Jennie anything, and my last letter from England to my mother told her to "watch the newsreels". She was an ardent picturegoer.

We were eventually freed from the boredom of West Kirby and taken in crocodiles across the Liverpool docks, and up the gangway onto our new home for the next few weeks; though on boarding we had no idea how long we'd be afloat or which ocean we might circle. But we had all been issued with tropical kit eventually — more weight for our kit bags.

The *Johann Van Olden Barneveldt* was a liner of considerable size with a Dutch and Javanese crew. There were many more male troops than female, and whether because of our supposed frailty or because there were so few of us we were shown to cabins with bunks. The men got hammocks on the lower decks.

On top of that privilege we were treated as first class passengers almost, along with the officers, by sharing the same dining room. After the food experience of the previous three years, meals aboard took on the appearance of a banquet each time we were seated. We were eight around a good round table, and the tiny Javanese waiters in their starched white uniform brought us food that would have pleased the palate of the most fastidious peacetime passenger. Or perhaps it looked that way in contrast to Britain's diet in the war years and for some time after; and I remember getting a real liking for kippers for breakfast.

I also remember how each time I was seated at table I was poked in the region of my right ribs by a short stubby finger. Funny how this sort always has that type of finger. This familiarity seemed to give much pleasure to one of the ship's officers, a fair portly fellow. He always strolled about at mealtimes, hands behind his back, except when he was poking, in a black uniform, examining that all were satisfied with the service. By the end of the voyage I didn't know whether to complain that he was wearing a hole in me, or to let him know I would have been vexed had he passed me without a poke. During the whole journey he spoke to me only once, yet I felt we knew each other rather well.

On first leaving port we had to spend each day well wrapped up. Even gloves and scarves were dug from kit bags to combat the fiercely cold ocean stream. Jennie and I had met Irene at West Kirby. She was a dark-haired, intelligent-looking girl who spoke southern English. A lovely lively person who became a constant companion to the end of my service days, and whom I still keep in touch with. We would mainly stand and talk to various Air Force men, usually finding out where each of us came from, and generally larking about to fill the endless hours between meals and sleep. In contrast to mealtimes though, we were happily allowed to share the biggest deck with the men of lower rank, while a smaller upper deck was out of bounds to segregate us from the higher ranks.

We could actually take quite long walks right around our own decks, and a shop was sometimes open, and a purser available. It was just as if we were taking a holiday aboard ship. Apart from the upper deck being out of bounds there were very few restrictions. The main one, and it was a vital one, was that we must never throw anything, not even a matchstick, overboard. And nobody ever did. Enemy submarines were ever alert.

After a few days we realised we were going much further afield than France however, and news had leaked out that we had somehow missed the convoy that was to escort us. Instead of going with the big one, we were given two destroyers of our own. It looked small protection in those dreaded days of disasters in the North Atlantic. To celebrate Christmas Day in our unusual circumstances the ship had placed a bag of sweets for each of us on our breakfast table, and it's surprising how a little thing can cheer one, when nothing is expected.

Soon the laughter began to fade from the ship, but it wasn't due to any fear of knowing we were in a vulnerable position, so much as the fact that seasickness began to take its toll. The packed body of uniforms got thinner on deck each day until there was hardly a soul to be seen except for the odd one who could find strength enough to stagger or crawl to the railings to vomit. We had been advised to keep food in our stomachs as long as possible, but I couldn't help smiling as I saw so many men take a grip on the railings while the gales flung the dreadful stuff back across their already green faces. The great heaving winter swells of the Bay of Biscay were living up to their bad reputation and what had started for most as a slight feeling of nausea, I'm told, became worse than the jaws of death. I sauntered forlornly on deck one day not even beginning to understand how so many humans could be dragged so low when I hadn't even the beginnings of the malaise. Could it be because the sea air had given me a feeling of well-being such as I had never known before? My appetite was superb, and I could hardly wait for the lovely musical chimes that invited, rather than demanded, we present ourselves for meals. I had to check myself from being a regular first at the table.

I was absolutely thrilled with the great heaving monster beneath my feet. I climbed as high and as much for'ard as I could and gazed with wonderment at the black and white of the Atlantic as it thundered against our bows. It drove itself upwards as if to wish me greetings on my high perch, then slid away to give a great dip to the ship. I loved the great power of nature battling it out against the invention of man but wanted neither to win. I felt the iron railings cold and firm as my eye slid with the ship to await happily the next great surge. I felt at one with the ocean, delighted as the spray reached my face, and try as they might, the few men left standing failed in their determination to make me sick.

I now wonder from whence they dug up such revolting stories which had obviously been invented for the very purpose. I've never forgotten one tale they tried on me. It was a tall, refined-looking boy who told it:

"A greedy regular went into a pub. His mates said, 'Hey Bill, if you drink some of the contents of that spittoon, we'll buy you as much beer as you want.' So Bill took up the challenge and surprisingly finished the lot. 'Why did you do that?' his mates asked, 'You only had to take a sip to win the bet.' Whereupon Bill replied, 'It was difficult to stop; it was all in one lump!'"

That was the sort of tale they tried to get me with, and it was at that point too that Finger-Poker spoke: "You are still here, that is very good. I'll sign you on for the navy." Gradually colour began to ebb back to pallid faces, though some never quite got over it. The decks were scrubbed down and we continued clean again, on through the Atlantic Basin.

One afternoon we were all out on deck as usual when the alarm sounded. This was immediately followed by an order, when a voice in clear precise tones said: "Attention please. Attention please. All personnel will put on life-jackets immediately. There is a submarine in our vicinity, and action will be taken. Return to your quarters immediately, then return to deck wearing your life-jackets and take up your emergency positions."

An immaculate silence had descended over all of us and we wasted no time in obeying orders. Fingers fumbled rather as we encased our shoulders in the bright yellow jacket with a small red bulb. I grabbed my water bottle and wasted no time with words. We returned to deck at once. An officer came hurrying past and told us: "Everybody find a spot where you can sit and brace your back against something solid, then don't move."

We quickly and silently did as ordered, and I found myself next to a slim fair girl who immediately bent forward across my knees and began to sob silently. In the next few seconds I decided there was no point in insisting she should obey orders. I put a hand across her back and she just kept lying there, rather awkwardly in her jacket. The deck felt hard and unrelenting against our bottoms as I remembered one instruction: "Don't switch on your lamp in the water until it gets dark."

We were hardly settled when the voice announced: "We are now going to drop depth charges, so don't be alarmed as the ship alters course. We are going to zigzag." His words were unmistakably clear.

I pressed hard with my back to assure myself that the outside of the cabin wall I was leaning against would take what was coming. The next second I saw the first of the charges as it was flung in a curving line from the portside. It looked like a rather large parcel I thought, but my mind was anything but clear.

The ship seemed to give a slight cough, then three more charges followed and I can remember simply thinking, "Thank the Lord I can swim, and if they don't shoot me in the water I am perfectly able to lie quite still and float as long as the water will let me". Then a picture of others unable to swim bothered me, and I gave a firmer grasp to the girl across me. I seemed to have forgotten what the life-jackets were for. I stared out across to the destroyer in my vision as I felt the ship pull away off course in a flurry of high knots. The light grey, smallish-looking destroyer did not give me much comfort, despite knowing one was on the starboard side too.

Absolute and uncanny silence followed the flinging of the depth charges and it seemed an age of silence as we stared gloomily across an otherwise empty sea. Then at last the voice, like a herald from God in the silence, spoke again: "Everybody relax. We think we've lost them. But stay in your jackets until further orders." But lurking inside us all was the thought that if we hadn't hit them, they must still be waiting and watching.

It was quite a long time before the feeling of doom left us and we could discard our jackets. It was a taste of what our aircrews must have been enduring, night after night, day after day, except that if they were hit, there was usually no ocean to jump into. The scare had given me much food for thought.

My charge at last arose and apologised to me, unnecessarily. I looked at her and smiled and that was all the understanding she needed. I looked further along and Jennie and I gave each other a reassuring little smile as we walked towards one another. At the time I was thinking how little I knew about ships. It had not occurred to me that we would be carrying weapons.

"Thank goodness that's over," said Jennie.

"Yes," I agreed.

Then Irene joined us saying, "I was looking for you. Where were you?"

It was a nice thought that she had wanted to die along with us, or perhaps give comfort to her soul as I'd done to the fair one.

"Well, I was looking for you too," I answered honestly.

It was apparent that real fear had silenced us all, as I noticed it had done to the German prisoners in hospital after which, relief makes voices temperate for quite a while, until fear at last loses its grip. We realised too, of course, that there must still be a great distance to cover. We were on our way to the Japanese sector of the war. We would become part of the South East Asia Command. For our part, as we were Air Force, we would become members of SEAAF.

At the time we left England, the war in Europe was looking much more hopeful for our victory. The war in the air had almost finished, although flying bombs were still reaching the south of England, a means of course of saving German aircraft and pilots. The aim now (which was the reason for so many personnel on our ship) was to keep up strength in the eastern war sector.

It was on June 6th 1944, six months prior to our departure, that the turning point was made in Europe. What could only be described as the greatest armada of ships and floats ever assembled had then left the waters south of our island and landed at points in France. It had been the subject of much debate between the high command — where best to land?

The Allies had by then achieved control of the air, thanks to the brave bomber and fighter crews of the allies, of whom about one third eventually lost their lives. Unfortunately many men had died on the landings, soldiers who had been held back specially to do the job, as had Eric's lot. On New Year's Day 1945 therefore, although great strides had been taken and many plans achieved, the Allied forces knew there was still plenty of fighting ahead, and not only in Europe.

As midnight struck at the end of 1944, a year in which I had had very mixed thoughts regarding my own destination in life, I drank a toast to the coming year with no sense of anything concrete in my mind. And that included love, work and home.

The whole shipload had been allowed to stay up. We had all assembled as much as possible, considering the space available, into one of the lounges. We were packed like matchsticks in a box. Irene, Jennie and I were together as usual, and were with some fellows, Jimmy and the rest, with whom we chatted a lot on walks about deck. A slim fair fellow then caught sight of us: "Jolly good show, I've been looking for you." He was squeezing his way towards us accompanied by good-hearted chaff. He had managed to get through to us carrying a glass full of sherry by means of his palm flattened across its top.

The three of us were allowed the tiniest sip apiece, and it was the only drink we saw before we took to our bunks later. I think we'd been privileged to a drink because we'd got into the habit of smuggling. Often after meals, we stole from the table with our serviettes bulging with a large lump of cream-filled gateau or some similar delight. These smuggled-out offerings were passed to the fellows, and each got his turn for a treat. We'd begun doing this when we happened to mention the wonderful banquets we were having, and how there was so much food we didn't think we'd last the journey devouring so much each day. It was on learning of their miserable lot in comparison, that we agreed to brighten up their diet, and this we did for the rest of the voyage.

After I'd sipped my sherry I was wondering where Eric was at that moment. We'd received no letters since leaving home, and I knew I wouldn't get one for some while. The longer I was parted from Eric, the more I began to wonder how I'd ever got engaged. Even so, I wished him a safe return from France at that moment. Apart from anything else, a mother who'd sent her son so willingly, jolly well deserved to get him back.

However, the events of the immediate future were to drive him even further from my thoughts. On that first day of January we little knew and would much less have believed, had we been told, of the life in store for us. The three of us were heading for things of which dreams are made — but dreams so often turn into nightmares, or at least badly let one down . . .

CHAPTER
TEN

Into Tropical Kit

As the days passed, the temperature crept upwards and upwards and, I am happy to relate that, the underwater menace had left us alone. By the time we reached Gibraltar we had donned our khaki-coloured tropical clothes. In our case this consisted of the usual A-line skirt and a rather pleasant long-sleeved shirt of Aertex material which both looked and felt nice though we usually wore our sleeves rolled up.

We replaced our "blackouts", a perfect description for our British all-weather bloomers, for some loose cami-knickers that each one of us had bought and packed. We cast off our lisle-thread stockings and from then on went bare legged. The long days suddenly became fit only for lounging on the well-trodden and sun-splashed decks. Of course there were no such luxuries for us as deck-chairs, but at twenty-one years of age I had no real need of comfort anyway. If only we'd packed a tennis ball and racket, but of course, the ball might have landed in the water! We must have packed colourful silk scarves too, because I clearly remember wearing one to stay my hair in the lovely warm breezes, as we took exercise when we tired of lounging.

It still amazes me to think of what we humped about over the years. This time, I had left behind my copy of Moffat's translation of the New Testament, for the sake of less weight, which the members of Wrekenton Chapel had sent me in the August of 1942. Jennie had also received a copy, for we had both been Sunday School teachers there. War had changed our priorities, but a moment came, later, when I wished I'd packed my copy.

It is surprising how love in a cold climate ever gets started or continues, for I recall that as soon as the sun struck across our ship, the men, and possibly the girls too, began to look for romance in all odd corners of the decks. Shipboard romances were as much in evidence on a wartime troopship as on any other ship that hits the heat. Although I was wearing an engagement ring, which had been noticed and actually mentioned, it did not seem to stop the fellows from trying. The shortage of girls made us all equally in demand; such a nice irregularity for us. The affairs though, were very much on the flippant side, not meant to be more than an interlude to while away time, and passing through the Mediterranean was a delightful experience, but we still did not know where we were destined for.

At Port Said we halted and got our first real glimpse of things foreign, for we three had not come from backgrounds with travel inherited. And here we watched as men, stripped to the waist and with only thin cotton trousers at calf length, showed chests of deep bronze, wore large gold earrings, and had colourful kerchiefs knotted around curly black heads. It was such an exciting scene, just as if we'd landed on a Hollywood set, and this was to be a sea adventure film. It quite thrilled our maidenly and over-stretched imaginations.

However, the stars of the scene were simply loading and unloading goods for the journey, but they laughed and chattered in a quick tongue, showing brilliant white, flashing teeth, and brought us our first glimpse of things to come. It was an Arabian-nights-like speck on our horizon. And here too, the Bum-Boats came alongside with their owners pleading for us to buy trinkets. Few did, because, as usual, money was short.

Then we began to pass through the Suez Canal towards the Gulf, and it was here that we got another brisk look into things foreign. The scene this time though was not quite a repeat of Port Said, but a sort of sinister aspect of things ahead — sinister in that we'd had no hint of the foreigners we may meet and perhaps live amongst.

The Canal itself prompted us all to stand and stare. We'd all heard of it and marvelled at its existence and now here it was, carrying us all along. In fact it appeared rather barren, land-wise and water-wise, and was simply a useful stretch of water as far as I could see. There was, however, a sudden and urgent flurry about us to see things or something going on. Jennie, Irene and I were standing of course, and being just girls, were that little bit shorter than the mass of men surrounding us. The disturbance aroused our interest too and we said words to the effect: "Come on then, let us see too." We hoped the men would move aside or lift us even, but there was an immediate attempt to sort of shuffle us backwards, a definite resistance to our viewing whatever had riveted the men's attention. That attitude of course made us even more determined. What on earth did they not wish us to look at? We reared on tiptoe sufficient to let us see, whilst the men squirmed at our insistence. There, on the barren banks of the canal, were six men in Egyptian robes, who were paired off into three couples, demonstrating what life was about to be like for men deprived of the female sex. Their sideways silhouettes were stark against a clear Egyptian sky. I'd never heard the word homosexual and knew nothing of such desires in men, but we were being given a demonstration of it on the banks of the Canal. There was nothing else in sight, and the men on our decks gave sudden low guffaws and low mutterings. It was therefore not surprising that those in our immediate vicinity had attempted to protect us from the sight, almost as if we'd been a girlfriend or sister. They were obviously unaccustomed to explaining a man's strange needs and they quickly drifted away quietly in a most embarrassed mood and three young English ladies were left to sort out the episode as best we could between us. We had no idea there were two different worlds of thought for men and women.

It was after we left Aden and got into the Arabian Sea that we learned where we were to land. It was to be at Colombo, the famous port on the west side of Ceylon, that dream island at the tip of India in the

Indian ocean, and which is now called by its previous name of Sri Lanka. As I got to know it when it was called Ceylon, so it shall remain in my story.

We still had no idea where we would be working, but where it was to be. It was a long way from the France I had volunteered for. I began to think there was something in the volunteering business after all, even if it just added up to long weeks of holiday at sea.

We'd had a wonderful rest, free from night duty and weekly inspections, and no annoyances at the marrieds getting first choice of leave dates. The voyage had been a blessed release from cold and hungry Britain. What was around the immediate corner we didn't really care, as yet.

By the end of our voyage we'd learnt a little bit more of life, and I'd begun to think a lot more life would reveal many more misrepresentations of it. Many of the things I was now learning, nobody had bothered to teach me.

We'd had a concert on board one night when typically, a frail-looking WAAF wearing glasses had been the only one to volunteer to give a turn. She'd boldly sung, "And it's oh that I'm longing for my 'ain folk . . ." and we'd all sort of gone into a kind of despair, a false acknowledgement for her. We weren't really sentimental; we weren't honestly missing home, not yet. We only had short occasional spasms of that. It was a great relief for all when she sat down after one song, though she got fair applause for her guts. Who but such as she would have dared against such a shipload?

100

We'd also had the inevitable lecture on board one day, just before we disembarked. We were told in no uncertain terms how to behave in the new land. The officer reminded us that in the Indian Continent we were regarded as masters. We gave the orders. It seemed we lowly ranks even, were to make a sudden transition from the roles we'd been told to play back home, where we'd always been the underlings. Yet much later, Irene and I experienced an incident that disproved the officer's statement.

We were told also that one must haggle over prices regarding shopkeepers, and this we found later was correct. They were the two main pieces of advice we received. We had been told nothing of the various religions, and that the majority of the Sinhalese people were extremely poor peasants. All this we would learn in the months ahead.

At last the day arrived when we had once more to pack our bags. The memory of the sea, of the jumping porpoises — one of the ballets of the sea — faces we'd got to know, like Finger Poker and all the rest, were laid gently away into the recesses of the mind.

As we entered harbour and dropped anchor I'm sure all, like myself, got a delicious kind of thrill. A colourful flag was gently caressing a vivid sky, and people with dusky skins in bright, white garb lazily stared up as we all gathered to work our way down the gangway. Being considered foreign, we were to get used to being stared at regularly, rather than people dropping on knees before us.

101

Then men were dispersed in one direction and our much smaller contingent in another. An officer accompanied us to our new quarters in Colombo and the first thing we all wanted was to have a good wash in nice fresh water. Weeks of washing and trying to bathe in the salt stuff had left us feeling decidedly sticky. Even the special soap we'd been given to combat the salt produced not one flake of lather.

As usual our quarters were bare except for beds and these were close together, but it transpired we were only to remain there temporarily. We did not learn immediately where our next move would be, but because we had been separated so long in England, Jennie and I had firm determination to try and remain together now. Irene too, now, had an equal desire to remain with us, which pleased us highly, Jennie and myself. We had thoroughly enjoyed her company the whole of the voyage, yet there was a secret and a sadness which she had not divulged to us, but we were to learn of it later as our friendship deepened.

As soon as we were all washed and settled, we were told about things we would be allowed to do while waiting for a posting. It was to be a further few days of holiday until they got our destinations sorted out. It was a short period that would introduce us to our new environment, a prelude to a whole new life.

CHAPTER
ELEVEN

First Stop Colombo

Next morning we arose early, which is what everyone wishes to do in Ceylon. As the day begins to shimmer in all its gold, the human pulse yearns to go out and meet life. It was little wonder that on our arrival we'd felt life already gripping us with a new excitement. As we'd watched Ceylon rising, from the railings of our ship, we already knew that the frozen codes of England were about to be left flapping away on the breeze. A new miracle had crept into our young souls. It was nothing to do with being so far from home and that therefore anything goes because, as I mentioned, we had already been lectured on behaviour. Anyway, we were already moderate and reasonable-thinking girls. It was simply that the climate and all it produced transformed the whole outlook of life immediately. For people from a cold climate, it stopped the thinking, arguing, worrying. It was a balm, which no other method has the effect of soothing one's being so completely. We had suddenly met bliss.

Colombo has been described as the most wonderful artificial harbour in the world, which must be near the truth. It is decorated by nature's wonders — palms, golden sands, and foam-flecked breakers. The harbour was filled with ships from the seven seas, liners, clean and majestic, rich men's yachts, catamarans with oars that balanced them as they danced on the ocean, and lots of interesting smaller craft. But all we had in mind at first was to go swimming. It had been rather a misery to me I recall, to have travelled thousands of ocean miles without being able, just once, to immerse my body in the tempting green. I am always so drawn to the sea I sometimes feel I was once a fish!

The OIC had collected us together early on that first morning and handed us some local money, and from then on we were handed our pay in a civilised fashion without parades. She explained briefly how to get to places and what to see. So it was with a sense of excitement that we hunted for a bus to take us the eight miles along the coast to Mount Lavinia. It was just the three of us. We had set off too with the warning to keep out of the sun at every possible chance. "Do stay in the shade," had been repeated several times, "you'll suffer if you don't!"

We enjoyed the drive itself, first along a great wide road, then through bazaars, past shops and through delightful streets lined with attractive houses, and like the rest of the world, they had churches. We missed no clues about our new world as we sped the miles, and we could hardly wait to see the sea either.

At Mount Lavinia we gazed about us in more wonder. It was difficult to say which had the most beautiful colour, the fine sand, the sea, the gently waving palms of trees, or the blue, blue sky. Only a

104

dozen or so were in the water. Some were dusky-skinned and some white men and a dusky male seemed to be persuading those in the water not to venture more than a few yards. Probably a coast guard, we thought.

We stationed ourselves under a palm for shade and each of us changed in turns while the other two sheltered her from stares, along with the trunk of the tree. It seemed we had all prepared ourselves by packing a bathing suit too. I'd fashioned my new one from a tube of light turquoise elasticated cotton that Eric's mother had obtained somehow. A bit of clever marketing I suppose. Clothes were hard to come by during the war and bathing costumes almost impossible. Our uncovered flesh, arms, legs and faces were already well bronzed from the voyage, but our bodies looked sickly. We stepped into the deep turquoise of the Indian Ocean for the first time with a feeling we were being christened. It was cooling, fantastic, and it was something that was to become a ritual with us.

The waves rolled in very high that day and were wonderfully tipped by foam. We discovered that there was indeed a strong pull of the tide. We appreciated then the warning gestures of the Sinhalese man. We spent half an hour in the water then went to sit under our palm, still feeling that it wasn't all quite real. I, at any rate, should have been breaking ice in France. Was heaven really so close? In the end we dragged ourselves away from paradise and returned to Colombo for our meal, full of excited talk with the others too.

105

We told the officer of the wonderful time we'd had, at her enquiry, and again she asked: "You did keep out of the sun?"

"Yes, we've been sitting under the trees," we told her, and Jennie added: "We really were careful."

But within two or three days our backs were really hurting. The short periods they'd emerged from the water while we bathed were enough to frizzle our skin. Unfortunately we had been given beds which had bases formed from rope knotted into largish squares and only one blanket each to lay on top of this. I think they must have been a rushed buy for our temporary accommodation with no mattress provided, so we spent the rest of our stay in Colombo face downward at night. Occasionally I felt myself being strangled chest-wise, and had to dislodge myself from a square. Heaven, we'd soon discovered, has its drawbacks.

We found ourselves walking rather erect around the shops thereafter, for even our light Aertex shirts hurt. However, it must have given the natives the impression we were very smart. Such bearing! This was just as well, for we noted that as they walked about very slowly in the evening, how truly elegant the Oriental women were. It must be their stature and bearing which gives rise to romantic fantasies by men of all nations. It was not surprising, when one saw them in their most beautiful saris walking a few paces behind their men. This habit of women always keeping a few paces behind also appeals to men of course!

We noticed that there were many healthy-looking businesses in the "Fort" area, and it would certainly be where much of the wealth of the island was. Notable was the ample figure of the Indian Chetty and moneylender, draped all in white. It was a cosmopolitan crowd we watched, a Malay in a striking sarong, sporting a batik cap at an angle, a be-turbaned Afghan with those funny baggy trousers and a velvet waistcoat, a red-fezzed Moorman, Tamils, Burghers, Muslims. Some, of course, preferred European outfits, so that we often saw a white suit topped by a white solar topee. The Sinhalese was outstanding by his black hair kept long and knotted at the nape with a tortoiseshell comb on the head, and attired in bright clothes, and often carrying an umbrella. Second to him was the Tamil in thin white with a white shawl. They all went to make up the intriguing Eastern scene.

One of the most striking features of Colombo life seemed to us to be the rickshaw-pullers. These were darkly bronzed men in what could only be called an emaciated condition, barefoot and often wearing little clothing. Considering the fact they ran about in such temperatures pulling both vehicles and people, it was not surprising that they had no flesh. In fact, they were a kind of taxi service for the city, though there were plenty of cars that taxied about too. Buses and tramcars also looked overflowing with humanity, and bullock carts trundled with equal rights to the wide roads. Colombo was indeed a scene of commerce, but apart from the rickshaw-pullers, people never ran.

In the cool of the evening, we found it delightful to stroll along the sea front opposite the world-famous hotel, the Galle Face, and while strolling we naturally met some British boys doing the same and again light romances whiled away time. Yet one felt that an arm placed casually across the shoulder as we sat gazing across the ocean was frowned upon by the locals. It seemed they had souls as spotless as their streets, or wished to give that impression. Proof of how light-hearted were the romances is that I cannot remember the name of the young man who walked with me and who later visited me when I'd settled in a camp. I am simply left with the impression that he smiled a lot. Neither can Jennie remember her partner on those occasions.

One morning a meeting interrupted our pleasure plans. It was now time to be sorted out, to be sent back to work which was why we'd gone in the first place, though the weeks of leisure were beginning to form into a habit. We three became very alert when the time came to allocate us all a camp. We waited impatiently as other trades were sorted out, but at last the officer was asking for three teleprinter operators for Koggala. Our hands shot up like rockets, as if she had asked for volunteers for a tour of Fort Knox when the sentries were absent. She looked a bit thoughtful at our eager response, we thought, but then agreed saying rather casually: "The camp is in the jungle, girls, OK?"

We glanced quickly at each other. "Yes," we affirmed. Then we grinned and smiled at our success. The officer's surreptitious warning had not sunk in. Like lambs once more we had fluffed up our wool and succumbed to suggestion, even though given a warning. It was a fact of course that we had survived more than three years healthily enough despite near diphtheria, bouts of diarrhoea and other minor irritations. We were indestructible. We'd always come up smiling.

CHAPTER
TWELVE

Lagoons and Baboons

Next morning we packed our bags again and awaited the transport to take us to Koggala. When it came, they were trucks with canvas coverings driven by RAF bods who gave us a welcoming smile. "Going far girls?" our driver commented in a playful manner. "Well how far is it?" We were more serious. "Only about eighty miles. I'll soon have you there."

He was as good as his word and drove at a mad pace that made the truck into a good rattler. It too was the first of many such rattling journeys to various destinations. In such thin skirts and much thinner underwear, it wasn't exactly the most comfortable of trips, though the canvas top and the draught of our speed helped to keep us cool.

We talked little on the journey because we were too busy, too fascinated, watching the scenes as we passed them, through the open back of the truck. Exclamations came though as a smelly village was passed, or a vision of beauty appeared in the form of a female or landscape: or even a few men at the water's edge brought a comment. They often wore nothing but a cloth about the groin.

As the miles fled by a sense of adventure prevailed amongst the girls. We were forty in number and when we reached camp it seemed a small army as we unloaded our kit on to a nice stretch of grass — a deceiving plot we discovered later. Snakes enjoy grass as much as undergrowth.

Ceylon we were discovering seemed well supplied with narrow roads considering the size of the island, 140 by 320 miles. From Colombo to Koggala we had trailed the coast most of the time, and much of the landscape had been bare of buildings. After the ancient fortress town of Galle, it had deteriorated, began to look wilder, and by the time we reached our destination we found ourselves in virgin jungle.

However, the grass had been part of the preparations for us, and because we were weak feminine mortals, they'd hewn down a few trees and on the tidy clearing they'd built a few long huts in concrete with pretty red tiles for roofing. A quick investigation revealed an ablutions hut too that contained both bath and shower room and a line of toilets. It all looked so cosy, so civilised, but that was just first glance. In the living huts we saw that fans had been fixed to the ceilings for cooling purposes. We found the usual furniture, beds; but this time there was an addition to them. Now we had mattresses, a pillow and two sheets. A lengthy stretch of white muslin-type material was also attached to each bed. It was pointed out that these were mosquito nets, and we must never lie in bed without them tucked firmly under the mattress, around every inch of it. The net was fixed from above the bed. And

111

though we'd be sleeping nude, the officer said, due to the excessive temperature, it was a spot of medical advice that we must always cover the loin area with the spare sheet. The main organs of the body we learnt were most vulnerable to any sort of draught, even warm ones, and the fans caused cooling draughts, or attempted to, we soon discovered. We were told that an Ayah would be arriving for us at our disposal, because of course it was not only tradition for whites to take servants on the Indian Continent, it was fairly necessary too. They could cope with the heat much better.

When we got ours later, we found she was called Helen, and she was fabulous, though not in the work sense particularly. She turned out to be as slow moving as any native; and sometimes she stole, but her looks and figure were sensational. She had the usual lovely long black hair parted centre and draped bun-wise onto her neck. Her complexion was like cream silk, her eyes huge brown orbs, but outstandingly on top of this her eyelashes were so long, and curved so delightfully, they almost seemed to float independently. What a pity she was an unconscious thief, because her figure should have put her in films. We first discovered her light-fingered streak when, one day, she came wearing a European dress. We noticed that a slip belonging to Evelyn, who'd been searching high and low for it, was hanging below her dress and she showed only slight concern when tackled on the matter. Perhaps because clothes always had an abandoned look in the huts, she thought they were anybody's for sharing.

112

On first arriving at camp, we were given a meal, after which we were called straight away to a lecture. This was also attended by a large number of RAF men. It was then that we learned about the various terrors that surrounded us. We must never walk barefoot, never go through the undergrowth without our legs protected and never risk the jungle at night, but if we had to we must carry a torch. Poisonous snakes were the main menace we were warned and not fussy who they attacked. We were advised that swimming was readily available. The camp area had obviously been specially selected. The jungle helped to give it more secrecy, and the coral reef at the coastal stretch in front of the camp formed an excellent safe bay for swimming. On the other side of the narrow reef though, sharks kept a watch for the unwary. It seemed we were placed between the devils of the deep, and the unknown devils of the jungle. Apart from that there were mosquitoes and these in good supply we were warned, though there was little we could do about them.

The Royal Air Force must have known exactly what it was doing when it drew up plans for WAAFs to be sent there, hence the special clause in the notes of the meeting, that came next. In stony silence we learned with sudden shock that we were forty against two thousand. In other words, there were forty WAAFs in camp now, but somewhere hidden in the lush undergrowth of that jungle were two thousand hungry men. It sounded an enormous figure. To simplify it, that meant we were outnumbered fifty-to-one — and for us that meant fifty-to-one *against*.

113

It was difficult to know at that revealing moment whether we should jump for joy, or flee back to Colombo and ask for another posting. The latter seemed preferable when the officer stated: "A lot of you men have been here a long time and we know that some of you have not set eyes on a woman for a long time. However, I'm sure we all welcome these girls who are from the homeland, remember, and are not here for your benefit, but to work like the rest of us. We ask you to restrain from the natural impulses, and that even wolf-whistles are out. Let these young ladies at least get used to the place first. Please behave like gentlemen. And in future you wear some clothes in camp!" I think we all froze for the first time in weeks. We, who were sitting near one another, looked to each other and then grimaced mildly. Would the males agree? It seemed at that moment that we had found ourselves suddenly in a domestic kind of war now, woman versus many men and that there were limits to good fortune.

We were then escorted back to our huts where our duty times were laid before us and from then on we were on our own. We told each other: "No wonder the transport Bods were galloping here with us." And we soon learnt that the "Brylcreem boys" were indeed eager for our presence.

Jennie, Irene and I were the only teleprinter operators there and had to cover every twenty-four hours between us. It meant there'd always be two of us off duty together, which pleased us. However, that day we were quite free to do as we wished. So, still with a sense of adventure, we stayed in our uniforms and

114

decided to explore the camp. From our own small clearing we set off, and to the rear of it we discovered a worn track through the high undergrowth, a nice clue that that direction might lead us somewhere interesting. We noticed that the palms were quite thickly clustered together, their trunks bending to struggle for more light, which, now fully grown, they were getting. Their heads formed a ceiling of fans. Between the palms lay sundry patches that formed very thick and healthy undergrowth. There were other trees too, strange to us, and ferns, much larger though than British ones, some like trees, which seemed about the only thing familiar to us. This was not surprising, as many plants of Ceylon are indigenous to that country; and then long, strong grasses struggled through it all too.

Although we walked slowly, we were soon sweating profusely, and we were discussing whether we would ever dare explore the undergrowth, when with a sudden shriek from each of us, we all stood rooted on the track. I who'd been walking in the middle of us, found two pairs of arms clutching either side of me. It was one short shriek before the three of us stood cringing and breathless, every muscle in our bodies taut with dreadful anticipation and our khaki uniforms quivered along with us. About three yards ahead, a monstrous creature was slowly emerging from the undergrowth. Its great scaly body kept growing wider as it inched its way forward on short legs supported by wide flat feet. As it advanced it was flicking a long thin type of tongue, forked with three prongs, and seemed to be using this as a warning to anything in its path.

115

We remained speechless and shivering against one another as fifteen feet of powerful jungle flesh seemingly ignored us then gradually disappeared with silent stealth into the undergrowth opposite, and at last even its tail went too. Its angle of appearance and departure had leaned away from us and we were glad about this, though none of us had spoken and said so; only our eyes had bulged with expression.

We had eased ourselves back as silently as the creature itself, out of tail distance especially, for we had already been warned to keep our distance from them as well as snakes. "One swipe," we'd been told, "of a Kabera Goya's tail can take off a man's legs." Ours were definitely thinner. I later saw a camp dog run yelping with pain or something, from the sting of one's tongue, one day too. The huge crocodile-like creature had, in those early hours at Koggala, been fair enough warning, and thereafter we walked with much obedience towards the dangers around us, which proved beneficial a few times later. We sensibly acquired caution from that moment.

Eventually that day we came to the important spot on camp. Set in the heart of the jungle area we suddenly came to quite a large lagoon. It looked delightful, but in fact was rather an unhealthy spot. Jungle lagoons look pretty, but harbour much that is unsafe to humans, and are delightful habitats for breeding mosquitoes. However, to us, that day, it looked most attractive. The surface was quiet and reflecting the azure sky in parts, and floating on it we saw a number of Sunderland transport aircraft. The white planes made it all look something like a millionaire's hideaway instead of a war base. Apart from the occasional rustle in the undergrowth, there was no other sign of life. It was like something imagined by H. G. Wells.

As we wound our way through more narrow tracks, we came across many small huts. They were erected from split trunks and palm leaves, and elevated from the ground, apparently to hold snakes, and other creatures, at bay. A small veranda made sitting around safer and pleasant for the occupants. With sweat soaking into our shirts, we stumbled back to our huts, grabbed towels and soap and absconded for the showers, something we found ourselves forced to do at least three times daily from then on. It was the only way to attack the heat, bar swimming.

In the ablutions block we found lizards happily cooling off too. They clung still and silent to the walls like some medieval decor or evil warning, but could suddenly dart off with amazing speed. We got used to them quite soon, though we had no choice about it. We got used to the native man too who forever stood lounging against the doorframe with a white garment draped from his waist to above his knees. Sometimes he must have found the energy to go inside and clean the ablutions, for they were seen to somehow. Neither did we have to get rid of our own STs any more. Considering the amount of time we spent in the showers, they ought to have hung pictures on the walls, though we never got bored with lizards. We were always wary about which way they might dart, and they took a long time making up their minds.

Another way to try and keep ourselves healthy was to drink as much as we could. I think I got my life-long love of soup at Koggala. I never got a taste for the sweet potatoes we were served, so I would fill myself up with seconds at the soup to provide me with more fluid. Salt had to be taken in large quantities also. In fact food became of less importance than hitherto, for nobody savours it too much in a climate just a few hundred miles from the equator. Fruit and coconuts and long cool drinks were the things we relished most.

We were too busy chattering in the huts that first night to realise what we were missing about six o'clock. I would always watch out for that time later, but that night the strange glow passed without our noticing it. But we did notice the mysterious sounds outside. First the crickets started, an interminable orchestra floating across the night, each chirping second dominating the senses, enough to send a person occasionally angry at their persistence. It was all to do with the disappearance of the sun then. The cloak of night brought many things to life, and in the minutes of twilight we heard the bending of branches accompanied by screeching sounds which travelled eerily across the blackness as baboons appeared to be rushing to find a resting place, the parents urging the young to hurry

We all just lay about and wrote letters that first night, to let the folks know we had arrived though of course we could not tell them where. But at least everyone back home would know we'd got there safely. Later a small black portable gramophone was produced by a girl named Evelyn, slim as a native, who wore about six very thin gold bangles on her arm; and very soon we looked forward to hearing her records regularly. She had a small selection of classical records and my particular favourite became Tchaikovsky's Nutcracker Suite, which still takes me back to Koggala whenever I hear it.

I recall now that these gramophones were a very important part of our war. There was always someone in the crowd who had one and once four of us played one for an hour on a train journey, entertaining the rest of the passengers, we thought, who anyway seemed to think it an enjoyable novelty, particularly when we produced "Old McDonald had a farm". Freda Dunn of Bradford will remember that journey, though she changed name when she married in a white lace wedding gown borrowed from Eric's sister. We had the whole carriage tapping, everyone smiling, which was fairly easy to do with wartime crowds; and the trains were always full.

We were tired, but I think blissfully happy that night as we tucked the nets under our mattresses, while we tossed around jokes of what might creep under them. Tomorrow it would be back to work at last, and soon we might get some mail, now that we were permanent once more. Letters were very important to all of us, and I found it an interesting fact during research to learn that Jennie's father never failed to write to her every week. Fathers are notorious for letting mothers get on with that sort of thing. Her sister told me: "Oh, my father was very proud that our Jennie was doing so much for the war. It was his most important job of the week to sit down and write to her."

It occurred to me then that perhaps my father too might have been proud had he lived. In fact I thought about him several times when I first arrived in Ceylon, of the tales he used to tell about his service in India. It had always seemed a never-to-be-achieved dream that I would one day see the land he spoke so lovingly about, and here I was on its very doorstep, and just like he did, loving it all too. My mother would not join him to live there after they married though. She once told me: "I didn't fancy living with all those natives." She must have had no sense of adventure and little humanity.

Apart from the bangles on our arms, which we'd now decided it was safe enough to wear, now that we'd "gone jungle" we all lay as Mother Nature had produced us. In fact from then on we never wore clothes unless we had to, which was only when we crossed to the ablutions or went outside to hang something on the lengths of string we used as clothes lines. But even then our garment was nearly always just a towel, which we'd tuck together by two corners.

If we flopped down exhausted after duty we might lie recovering in just bra and panties or a cami-slip. We only dressed for duty. It was much too exhausting to begin to feel shy about each other's bodies. We instantly became like the natural children of any hot lands where clothes are just a burden, though in Ceylon it was surprising how much the natives did cover themselves, unless they were very poor.

The dark sky that blanketed the Indian Ocean was all we ever needed for sleep, and the hand of God, which seemed so close there. That night was the beginning of a period that changed my whole life, just as it was to change Irene's too.

CHAPTER
THIRTEEN

Work & Fun Begin

The signals section was quite a distance from our huts. It was built like the men's huts, of split trunks and palm leaves with open spaces where windows would normally be in a cold climate. In our small room there were only two teleprinters, a great reduction on the number I looked after in operations at HQ. We had a mechanic to service the machines, who was sometimes hard to find, and one day I thought, "Have a look yourself and see if you can fix it", when one went U/S on me. I lifted its cover to find a mass of small intricate parts, and to my amazement seemed to know where to look for the trouble and found that the machine worked again. It was either good luck or woman's intuition.

Adjacent to ours was another smallish room where the radio bods worked. I could hear them tap tapping but could not see them as I worked, as the aperture connecting our rooms was too high as I sat working.

I remember getting to know the Praying Mantis well on duty. There always seemed to be one hanging around in the small area. It was a large insect roughly similar to a Daddy-Long-Legs, and it had the strange habit of appearing to continually pray as it clung to the wall, usually just above my head. "Say a good one for me," I remember saying to one on one occasion. No windows and the lights we worked in at night attracted them of course. I found them less frightening than the cockroaches we often found lurking in our shoes in the mornings. I, along with everyone else, got into a habit of banging out shoes before we wore them. To this day I still occasionally wonder if there is something in my shoes as I pick them up.

In the evenings a fruit "Wallah" would often be seen near our works section. This was a native with a cartload of fruit that was happily pounced upon by everyone. He brought a good selection including the most delicious pineapples, all so very cheap there of course, and carried bottles of fruit juice too. We bought ourselves supplies from him for our beach parties

We soon learned that we must only buy what we needed immediately, otherwise the heat ate it up first. Irene and I bought a pineapple between us one night and hung it in the curtain by our beds, thinking it would keep better hung up. We'd planned to eat it on waking. Next morning all we found was a mass of slush and a big sticky stain on the curtain. Lessons come quick and fast in the tropics. Mistakes there get no second chance.

Working alone got rather boring at times, especially when it was remembered how the other two would be enjoying themselves and the nights particularly seemed to drag, although we had the blessing then of feeling so much cooler. Off duty, people were either flopped on their beds to restore their energy which the climate played havoc with, or lay on the beach and went into the sea at regular intervals to cool off.

Our first two days at Koggala the men behaved as they had been asked. We were in fact startled to discover that many of them, due we suspected to their lack of contact of any sort with women for so long, were actually behaving quite shyly. If they found us approaching they hung their heads as if they had no right to look upon such creatures. Or perhaps the lecture had made its impact better than we expected. It was quite astonishing how some behaved. However, there are always the wolves, and these lost no time in getting us organised for their benefit, one way and another. That was how on the third night a dance was arranged.

We, the WAAFs, were offered a polite and proper invitation, as if they, the RAF bods had been dancing all along, yet the nearest thing to females we could see there were the monkey population. But, we were glad of the chance for some sort of entertainment and decided these things were necessary in such a spot, even on a wall-less floor in the wild. It was a cheering prospect as we donned our khaki.

It seems that the fellows had already decided that to give each fellow his chance, each dance should be an excuse me. It turned out to be quite a ridiculous idea. The gramophone played: usually six men at least made a grab at the nearest WAAF to them. We had to admit they'd done their best to appear gentlemanly, but, the second that the winner got us onto the floor, the next man was already standing ahead of us with arm outstretched to tap the already lucky man and get his turn. Each man allowed the last one or two steps, so that it turned into a game of "tag" and we girls just stood in the end and curled up with laughter unable to dance. The poor starved fellows — all they needed was to just touch a female. If they had all lined up, and each WAAF had gone along shaking each by the hand I think they would have been equally delighted. Dances, it transpired would either have to be by ticket or not at all.

The best companionship the men got from us was on the beach. Here, everybody could join in the fun. Sands surround the island, and the stretch fronting the camp was long and narrow and fringed at its rear by coconut palms. There was often a native standing, simply watching, but also ready to race nimbly up a palm and throw us down a coconut for a few cents. He would slash off its outer green skin for us with a very sharp knife, then break a hole for us to drink from. They'd also provided us with a palm-leafed changing hut, though it never got used from what I saw. Everybody just walked to the beach in sandals and swimwear. No doubt before our arrival the men would not even bother with swimwear. The girls naturally came off worst by the sea. We were often thrown bodily into it, dragged about to drowning point and chased around until heat overcame pursued and pursuers. Then we would all lazily float to cool down again.

The sands were burning hot and of a beautiful fineness and colour. The reef sometimes extended itself and formed delightful rock pools, and we watched, like

125

children round a pond, as fishes of every hue traced playful patterns for us. Some had those wonderful flash-bulb eyes which appeared to blink on and off as their owners wove about in figures of eight, or darted quickly by. In the bay itself we'd find ourselves swimming among shoals of darker fry, and one day Irene and I were captured and some handfuls of these fish were unceremoniously dropped down into the back of our costumes. We shook and wriggled to dislodge them but two still dropped out of mine after I'd returned and stripped in the hut; dead by then of course.

On first reaching Koggala our backs had begun to grow new skin and we could peel the rotten stuff off in great strips from shoulder to waist if we did it cautiously. Yet in a few weeks we were bronzed and hardened to the sun as much as the natives, though some people never bronzed. We felt heartily sorry for them and their red skins, for Irene, Jennie and I were all dark types whose skin lapped it up. We lost every spare morsel of flesh too for it just melted away. It was true what one male told me: "You look like a bunch of goddesses."

Jennie and I also recaptured a little bit of our teenage years. We had been accustomed to performing acrobatics in our extreme youth. We discovered when we were about ten that we could each do tricks that only a supple spine would allow and became a team performing at school and other concerts such as the church and the Rangers. Now we found the sands an ideal mattress and rediscovered our talent and found we could do all our tricks still. I was always the larger and stronger who could throw Jennie about, and at first the others would gasp and imagine we were about to kill ourselves. In consequence we not only became very wiry, our muscles hardened too.

We also tried trick dives, along with the men, each of us trying to outdo the other, but I fell foul of my image one day when we discussed diving without hands. I was the first to have a go and although I succeeded I resurfaced, with my nose grazed and bleeding as it had struck the coral beneath the sand. We would stand on the reef itself to make our dives, being careful not to go too near the dangerous side.

We'd been advised never to neglect a coral wound so I presented myself at sick-bay. The medical bod laughed when I said how I'd got my injury and was about to paint it with iodine when I noticed it was the brown stuff. At the same instant Jennie reminded me we were invited to a dance at a naval base that evening so I turned down the offer to be painted. My nose fortunately healed without trouble, and my Godmother's powder was used to camouflage the scratches for that night. I must have looked strange with a powdered face against such a bronzed body.

Of course, once the word got around that a bunch of WAAFs were near enough to be transported to their depots, we got invitations from far and wide so that our own camp fellows were forced to share us. Life at times became quite complicated with which ones to accept.

On the night of the first dance at camp a young Irishman had attached himself to me. Then, like a child

127

with a new toy, he'd taken me to meet a friend of his. I'd gladly accepted the offer to walk there with him, just to get away from the hordes at the dance. He took me to a house (if it could be so-called) that in truth was like an enlarged camp hut. It had a front veranda with two benches and a small table. It must have been the only house for miles before the camp was built; such a paradise for the owner, whose name, I think, was Mr McCready. He was sitting smoking a pipe and greeted us with much pleasure on our arrival then asked his houseboy to offer us drinks. I learnt that he lived there by himself, and had lived there for years. Nobody had bothered to shift him, they'd just built the camp around him and it seemed to have become a delight to him. He would entertain anybody who fancied making him a call.

After that night I saw little of my young Irish friend, though there could well have been a reason. About the third time I went on duty, I discovered another Irishman. I was dutifully busy at my machines when a head popped through the small adjoining aperture from the radio-ops room.

"Hello," it said, "I hope you don't mind me asking, but how do you like your men?" It was such a friendly voice, the eyes so blue, the hair so dark, that I answered mainly in fun,

"Mm, I think, tall, dark, and not too handsome."

He laughed: "I just fit the bill. How about a swim tomorrow?"

We did swim together, and from then on I somehow became known as "Paddy's girl". It just happened,

128

quiet-like, and in a way I looked upon Paddy as my protector from all the others, for he was tall I discovered, rather than anything more, quite tall enough to frighten the wolves.

I'd received a letter from Eric and all he could talk about was the war ending and being together. I found it a struggle to write any agreement to that back to him, but I kept on writing as if things were the same. I lived with a fearful thought uppermost in my mind, that if I wrote him the truth, he might deliberately get himself killed or something stupid. The thought of anyone else so close to me being killed upset me. I'd already had one closely associated death at the beginning of the war when a charming friend had been blown up in the engine room of his ship, a battleship. I was very young at the time, but it did something to me. I always felt I never wanted to feel too close to anyone again. For a long time anyway. That episode in my life was still haunting me, even then, though I never told anyone. I had a sense of blissful freedom at Koggala and I wanted it to stay that way.

We all took trips into Galle and bought ourselves things from the open-fronted shops there. I think everyone got sandals for comfort, the native type with a strap between the two large toes. I also ordered a pair of white calf shoes to be made with a view to looking smart when I took to civvies. We discovered a local woman there who was a genius at making clothes if we took her material. She would invite us into her home. Irene and I went one day and she handed us a fruit saying: "How many sections d'you think that has?"

"Mm, don't know," we said looking puzzled. Then she pointed out the scallops, and said the fruit would have the same number of sections as the scallops on its top. She invited us then to eat the fruit. She was the only Sinhalese we ever had a real conversation with. The fruit was a mangosteen. The kindly lady lived in quite a large house that was completely surrounded by a veranda high above ground.

One more friendly approach we had was from the camp "Dhoby" to whom we sometimes went to collect laundry. He invited us to look at his laundry when he saw we were peeping into it. It was just a ramshackle type of corrugated tin hut in camp, and we saw that six men sweated in the building, lifting absolutely enormous irons, which were hollow, and they were filled with red-hot cokes. The owner, who was obviously very proud of his business, invited us to try and lift one, which we barely managed.

His employees were extremely skinny, but looked eager and happy to show us how easily they could use them. However, our officer, who always inquired where we were going or where we'd been, ticked us off for going in, when we explained our little adventure. It had seemed harmless enough to us, but perhaps the fact that one of our girls had been attacked by a native one night, which caused them to put railings around our enclosure, warned her to caution us. On the whole we found the natives either too silent, those who worked for us, or over-friendly if we approached them, which was usually when we bought from them. I suppose they were simply as curious about us, as we were about them.

One day Irene and I had an idea. Though we had a camp hairdresser, our shift work rather hampered us from getting hold of her, and by now our hair was definitely beginning to look jungle too. All the heat, so much swimming, well, the lovely coiffured creatures which had left England were looking more like Tarzan's Jane, had Jane really looked her part on the screen. I think too, we missed the feminine habit of actually booking an appointment at a hairdresser's.

There was a barber's hut for men on the camp. We talked it over with the others and as Irene and I had suggested it, we were voted first to try the experiment. We'd approach the barber to see if he could give us a hairdo. It was pure rebellion on a camp with so many men. We braved ourselves and went, wondering would we just be glowered at? The barber was a wavy-haired creature himself, and when he heard our request his business impulses bristled: "Yes lady, I do the hair for lady. My father was one who had a proper ladies' hairdressing. Come and be seated." He was smiling like a benign uncle while the male customers gaped with interest rather than looked disturbed at our invasion of their premises. There were no multi-sex services outside of bedrooms in those days.

We knew that a few of the girls were peeping with curiosity from behind another hut following it all with interest too; so with a great pretence of confidence Irene and I seated ourselves. "Trim, wash, and set, please," we suggested. We knew it would be ludicrous to

131

ask for a perm. The barber worked away at us while I sat with my fingers crossed. The temperature in the hut was enough to dry our hair without a machine, of which he had none, of course. After about half an hour we emerged and could hardly contain our laughter till we got out of sight. Oh, he had done the job well, so perfectly in fact that he saw us off the premises with great aplomb, hoping no doubt to boost his business with more ladies. Mr Harichandra sent us out of his hut-shop perfect examples of fashionable ladies of the early thirties, bobbed and waved with one large quiff falling onto our foreheads. To him a marcel wave was still high fashion.

All the time we'd been sitting the girls had been watching as if it was a picture show. In such circumstances of everyday life though, with no entertainment, it was as good as such. We got our money's worth in laughter at the outcome of the experiment, but poor Mr. Harichandra got no more lady customers. In fact there had been no mirrors in the shop and until the girls handed us a mirror we did not realise how we looked ourselves. Only how we had seen one another.

Before long, a concert was arranged; the typical army-type, but now WAAFs could be used to partner men and a sort of Fred Astaire-Ginger Rogers type of act which I think was supposed to give a bit of real glamour to the show made me simply want to giggle. I can still see Jennie in long green slinky satin, but at least the men in the audience did not titter. Lots were due to go round the bend anyway. Of course with so

132

many men there had to be a sexual inference somewhere in the show, which in fact began by someone on stage saying: "Will all the men sit with the long leg over the short one please." That had been good for a titter. The show was one of the brave attempts to keep the troops from dying of boredom of course. Regrettably, after I'd left camp, Peter Sellers and Company entertained there, I learnt from Jennie.

An American naval base along the coast got wind of us too, and as usual with Americans during the war, they had much to give. Several of us accepted an invitation and we were seated at long trestle tables actually covered with cloths, and the tables were almost bow-legged with food and drink, then we all danced; and after that had to watch our step. They were, after all, a very healthy bunch. At that time America was not exactly leaning towards the idea of helping the British to continue the Raj in India, I have since learnt. There was a fair amount of disharmony in Anglo-American relations out East. It seems as if all the Generals were playing around with tensions of their own as much as war tensions at the time; and while Slim had been worrying whether he could get Rangoon before the monsoons burst, Mountbatten was doing his best with his manpower problems and trying to keep up our strength in face of the Americans. It seems a bit of a giggle now that the American troops were in no way being stuffy about the female British troops. They were welcoming us with more than open arms. Jungle boredom also became laced with almost vicious

133

excitement at times, especially for the girls. Man needs woman, and WOW!

I remember writing home saying how well we were being entertained and mentioned the lovely food we were getting on occasions. Once, somebody even gave us each a photograph of tables spread with lots of fruit that I sent home. Looking back, it was a cruel thing to do when I remember how miserable the food position was back home. My intention however had been to let my mother know she must not worry about me.

It was a fact that men were demanding our company so much, I think we began to sicken of it a little, and I remember having a serious discussion one afternoon with a fair girl. We both agreed that despite all the men we were meeting, somehow neither of us had been "caught up" in admiration with any one in particular. Yet it was not very long after that, that I made the most serious decision of my life about one that had not yet arrived on the scene, and I astounded my discussion partner with so doing. I think I probably astounded myself too, though it was much later that the thought occurred to me.

However, time passed and took on a never-ending perspective I think, so I got small surprise one day when Irene said: "Let's get dressed up, just as if it's a summer day in England, and we'll go for a walk." This is the sort of mental give-away that the heat is beginning to get one down. As soon as she said it I got the same sort of longing that she must have been feeling. How long was this sort of life going on?

She put on a pretty-coloured crepe dress with some white beads as if she were about to go to Tahiti. I too put on a crepe dress in a nice shade of brown with a gilded leather leaf-brooch, and put on my gold bangle that had begun to get a battered look as I'd been swimming with it so much. We set off eastwards, looking rather as if we had decided to go to church or at least a church fair, but we made our way into the jungle. It turned out to be a very interesting afternoon, and in more ways than one. It wasn't just the heat that had made Irene suggest a walk I was to discover.

CHAPTER
FOURTEEN

Secrets in the Jungle

The afternoon that Irene and I set off on our walk started differently somehow. There was a humidity in the air we'd never experienced until then. The sky had darkened somewhat, though it did little to cool the person. We picked our way carefully, and as we went, a truly lovely sound came through the trees to reach us. It was something like a flute, a pretty sound, and spreading itself with carelessness through everything about us. The oriole was entertaining, while the silent creatures listened. It was equally unconscious of the pleasure it gave to man or woman also. What delight a bird can bring, I remember thinking.

Sometime later we had the thrill of seeing a quite large snake which we took to be a cobra, but we hurried off feeling scared and left the thing in peace. It was much larger than the thin dark type which Jennie and I had almost trodden upon one evening as we were leaving my hut. That was truly frightening in that we had never expected it to be quite so near the entrance. We'd been just about to step on it when we caught the movement in the dim light from the hut, snaking its way within inches of us. That was the sort of thing a net was useful for. When we'd described it to admin there had been an immediate rush to get it and kill it; for what we'd described had been a very poisonous snake.

Eventually our walk took Irene and me to a less dense area, and it was then that the secret Irene had been holding back was revealed. There had been moments when I thought she looked deeply serious, but I'd ignored the expression as a mood. Living on top of one another, never being able to feel alone had its disadvantages. Often a girl would look in a dream as if she was thinking of something very far away, and nobody would then disturb her thinking. We all suffered from the claustrophobia of people at times. Girls in particular have days in the month when they feel the need to be alone. We could sense it in one another like sisters must.

I don't know what prompted Irene to tell me that day, but she seemed glad of the chance, I realised. I learned that she had volunteered to go abroad for a very solid reason. She told me: "I'm married." I frowned at her questioningly, so she began to pour out her story.

She had married a man in England who had neglected to tell her he was suffering from a serious illness that eventually caused him mental problems. He had disregarded the fact she ought to be told though he was still getting treatment for it when they married. She couldn't understand it when his behaviour became very unnatural, and in the end unbearable to live with. Being in Ceylon was her escape from something she never wished to go back to, though he was in fact still her husband.

I realised she was very unhappy and gave her what sympathy I could, telling her I was sure she would find something again to bring her back to happiness. She was reluctant to answer.

"Anyway," she said eventually, "It's been lovely to find someone I can talk to about it." I was glad I seemed to have helped. I told her nothing of my own emotional doubts of that time. Hers was a much greater problem than my own.

She was soon able to throw off the mood however that day as we ventured further and came upon a small building in the unspoilt area we'd reached. We approached it cautiously because of the strangeness of its location. On the opposite side to our approach we found an open doorway and looking in we got the surprise of our lives. Centred in the small building was a large statue leaving little room for anything else. The bubbly shape of the God Buddha stood in front us giving us a benign look at our surprise. The tiny temple (which was surely placed there for weary travellers, perhaps to find solace) looked so inviting, that we went in after we had glanced about to make sure there were no snakes. It seemed a sort of omen that we'd found it, since Irene had just released her secret. Was someone or something wishing her peace?

We touched the statue, which felt unusually cold, then discussed the fact that it was the religion of some of the island people. Neither of us then knew much about it, but their God looked quite a loveable being.

On returning outside we also noticed a bright scarlet flower not far away in the undergrowth. When we reached it, we saw there were two of them, a kind of beautiful orchid, luckily one for each of us. Paddy had twice brought me one I remembered. He'd told me: "Flowers disappear so quickly in the tropics. I was lucky to find it," when he brought me the first. It had pleased me more than the most expensive bunch of bought flowers would. Some species in Ceylon are truly rare and can have as long as five, six, or seven years between flowering. Irene and I picked them, then for some reason obscure to me she said: "I know, let's give them to Buddha." We re-entered the temple and for lack of somewhere more suitable, we placed the flowers on top of his flattish head. Pleased at the idea, we then left him, and I think we both felt that we had been most respectful to someone else's God. How many others had ever offered him flowers?

We came away quite happy, but before we reached camp again we were not too sure we had done the right thing; for what happened next, could have been considered a small punishment. We had decided to return by the coastal road, but unexpectedly we found ourselves putting up with an absolute deluge of rain. No one had warned us, but it was May, the month when the monsoons coming from the south-west bring their deluges with them. We got into a panic, but not just because of the rain which had soaked us immediately to our skins. The trouble was that both our dresses had shrunk instantly also. The crepe they were made from was the type that normally shrinks when

139

washed, and only returns to normal size when ironed out again.

We had to make our way back to camp absolutely soaked, and with our now tiny dresses clinging like a strange second skin against our slim bodies. Our hair was wringing wet too. We could hardly run in our effort to reach camp quickly because we were laughing so much. It was a funny end to a rather serious afternoon, though we managed to get into camp without being seen by any of the men. The girls howled at our appearance when we entered the hut. "Two wrung out sponges," was what someone said we looked like, even though we were dripping.

That same night, we got a further soaking from the rains, but this time it happened while we were in bed. Quite suddenly a great gust of the monsoon whipped off a lot of the pretty red tiles which made up our roof and ceiling combined, and the rains came slanting in. We were lucky that none of us got cuts, for the tiles were broken all across the floor Fortunately the centre of the roof had caught it worst, being the highest point, but some of us got wet. Our WAAF officer came racing across on hearing the news, to make sure we were all okay. She was always dutifully worrying about us. I'm sure the pretty young thing must have ended up with an ulcer too, she seemed to worry so. However, she found us all just looking rather surprised, and next day we discovered that all the palm-built huts, too lacking in comfort supposedly for our use, had stood up to the winds magnificently.

I should have been dreaming of black snakes and puff adders that night, and deluges of course, but I think we all had slept rather well afterwards because of the cooling conditions of the monsoon, and "wakey-wakey" time next morning was still buzzing with our experiences.

It had taken only weeks of course before the first fever cases started. Despite all our inoculations, vaccinations and immunisations, we went down one by one. I think Jennie managed to be the first to go into hospital. They had regular ingoings and outgoings. It was just as the families of the Raj days had suffered, though thankfully none of us died that I know of; for the white man quickly becomes subject to all the miserable ills that the tropics provide. Malaria, yellow-fever, dysentery, heat stroke, lumps and bumps from bites; anyone who escaped the lot was indeed lucky. And the nasty prickly heat was the commonest curse, though I never got that.

A young, ginger-haired sprog arrived to replace Jennie on duty until she was well, and I couldn't help smiling at his concern at having to leave his girlfriend back home. I recalled that one male on camp had announced to me that he didn't want to return home to his wife, since she'd become a cripple having their child. He told me he couldn't see much of a future for them. Life was proving very confusing for me the more I listened to men. I suppose young ginger changed too, later.

I was contradicting myself of course by keeping company with Paddy so much, though we did little

141

beyond swimming together and joining the groups who made up beach parties. This was nothing more than going to the sands, perhaps just before sunset, our arms full of good things to eat and drink. And inevitably the black portable gramophone assisted everyone to get the full mood we intended for wriggling our toes in the sand.

On the nights that we went there early we got the best entertainment that the world can give. About six o'clock each evening it happened. The most glorious sunset trickled its way across the vast area above the Indian Ocean. It might begin with gold splashes, there was no guarantee, and then it emblazoned itself with every beautiful hue. It formed truly magical pictures, and the blinding splendour hypnotised all that watched it. I always had the feeling that if God had settled somewhere, then that island was where he must be, and it was He who unfolded such magnificent dreams before us. Second by second the majesty changed and He would send scarlet devils fleeing through purpled entrances into caves of heavenly blue. Then shapes that resembled drifting ballet dancers in pink and canary yellow would glide over turbulent aquamarine waters. And then, in the great silence of it all, for no one ever spoke, coloured rockets would suddenly shatter the whole, and explode it to a fountain of rainbows chasing green bats that darted amongst curling turquoise monsters. Then at last there appeared the stillness of great darkening mountains which quickly melted to a realm of complete darkness. The ocean came to rest, having sucked in the reflections it had played with, and on land the crickets started their orchestra. The baboons would be the last to screech about it all.

We'd been lying one night, Paddy and I — with others — watching this spectacle, when Paddy suddenly leapt to his feet.

"What on earth's the matter?" I asked. He was backing away as if being approached by an army of snakes, but when I looked across to where his eyes were pinned, all I saw was a crab; but I had to admit it was quite a monster. It was staggering sideways on the verge just at the back of the sands. Then another shape began to move too. Occasionally we'd seen a tortoise like this. I sadly accepted that my great protector was as unreliable as the rest of men. I could have accepted his getting out of the way but it was the way he'd left my side so quickly without a thought of pulling me with him. I'm still looking for a St George to this day. All the dragons I've known have been left to me to fight on my own. It's the tiny unacceptable act that can put a girl off a man quite easily.

It was in May too of course that we learnt that the war in Europe had ended, and happily with our victory. May the eighth might have been a time of celebrating in Britain, but it had no impact on us, so far away. Looking back, it is the one event I am sorry I missed regarding the war. I'd have joined the singing with gusto.

I received a letter from Eric's sister to say they had nominated me by proxy as Godmother to their new daughter. Dennis had become a father, Marilyn Janet, my new Goddaughter. And about the same time I also became an auntie, and little snaps arrived to show what I was getting. Birth keeps on happening, despite all disasters.

It was my turn next to get fever, and I recall being piled with blankets, or that's how it felt since I'd got used to sleeping without the weight of even one. I was ushered into the camp hospital weak from head to toe. They were quite kind. I was mostly lying alone that time, though occasionally someone gave me a short visit. Nobody made prolonged visits since so many got fever. It was accepted that we put up with it and suffer in silence. If it wasn't fever it was something else. However, we hoped not to get malaria because of its repetitive attacks throughout life. Nevertheless I had continuous ill-health for years after I returned home, and on one occasion whilst having an investigation done at a hospital in England, they asked if I'd ever been out East. This made me wonder if they'd found something strange in my bloodstream, or perhaps something missing.

My complaint while having fever however, was not against anything the nasty little mosquito had done and caused; but that I was supplied each day, twice a day at first, with chicken and wondered why. When I commented upon the repetitiveness of meals, I was almost sulkily told: "But you're very lucky. The Red Cross supplies us especially with them for you sick ones." Being the only patient that week I was getting spoiled with the lot, apparently.

It was true of course in those days that chicken for dinner was considered a luxury in most British homes. They were something special at Christmas. But to have it every day and in fever-throes, did not appeal to my appetite and I begged for fruit. Chicken did appeal to us though, when it was wrapped in yellow curry. To get it we sometimes went along to one of the rest houses where this was served and it made a pleasant change from camp food. Rest houses are usefully dotted around the island and are just what they describe, a building, usually wooden in structure where one can rest, eat and drink, and be quietly merry.

Curry of course is most suitable to the tropics. They need a lot of it because it's the one thing that disguises the rot when food is beginning to turn putrid. Without curry, heaven knows what else people would get on top of malaria, yellow fever, dysentery and the rest.

Despite illnesses, between the three of us we somehow managed to keep the teleprinters working and the planes kept ferrying people and supplies back and forth to the fighting front. But one day there was quite an uproar in camp when it was discovered that the natives working there had somehow been using our planes for smuggling. What they were smuggling I never found out. Perhaps it was jewels, for which the island is famous. However, in the large flying boats with their roomy interiors and more than one deck, it was probably quite easy for the natives to find useful holes to bury things away. These Flying Boats, Class VI in the category of aircraft, were the only planes which the women of Air Transport Auxiliary, the ferrying pilots

I'd wanted to join, were not allowed to fly. In actual fact there was a height limit for the ferry pilots which I did not reach anyway — five-foot five, I seem to remember.

One day our officer called a group of us together. She must have felt duty-bound only to suggest it, and we began a game of passing the ball, or netball, without the net, but it only lasted minutes. Anyway there was no proper sports ground, and just darting about in the grass seemed a little ridiculous. In no time at all we were feeling rather faint, fleeing about in temperatures fit to scurry lizards into the loos. Besides, so much swimming had us near Olympic health, we did not need scorching with ball games.

Weeks went by with us hearing just about nothing of the war, and even the songs we occasionally caught each other humming, began to sound dated too. They held no relevance to our state of life, and soon faded from our lips in the same way marriage vows lose relevance so quickly. The "White Cliffs of Dover" began to sound promisingly cool to us rather than a visual tribute to victory. And "Roll Out the Barrel" sounded far too energetic in the east despite the implication it would quench a thirst which was one of our principal needs then.

We had become much more inclined towards Evelyn's classical mixture on her gramophone. The sweat of the tropics did not mix easily with tunes such as those we had sung in chorus in our huts back in England. Songs such as "Pistol Packin' Momma, Lay that Pistol down", or "Mairsy Doats

146

and Dozy Doats". In actual fact we were losing touch completely with any new publications of songs, almost losing touch with reality in many senses. We had no radios, nothing, and the regular weekly dances we had attended back home, which kept us in the song picture, were not available in Ceylon. Of course we did have our trips in the "Passion Wagons" — trucks used to carry us to invited outings and which often took us to places where the musicians, if any, were still clutching to the old favourites for the same reason as ourselves. In fact many of the men had left home some time before us.

We all felt rather unhappy when we learnt that one of our WAAFs had become pregnant, though she did not appear so herself and she refused to be sent home on compassionate grounds, wishing to stay with her man. I never heard the end of that story, and it was my first hearing of an unmarried WAAF becoming pregnant in almost four years.

Another WAAF gained our sympathy because she always seemed troubled with prickly heat, while another was permanently covered with lumps from some sort of bite. We thought it interesting to realise how some insects took a particular fancy to some types of flesh, and the rest of us were just glad it did not apply to ours.

Suddenly in June, a lot happened; things that were to alter my own personal life, and which also started a chain reaction in Irene's too. Jennie at the time was quite enjoying a mild friendly affair of her own, but suddenly looked happy to take a hand in arranging my life. June was to be a month I suppose I'll never forget followed by a more important one in July.

CHAPTER
FIFTEEN

A Message from the Past

At the end of May Paddy learned that he was to be repatriated. It was a small blow to my life, simply because I felt sure it was his presence beside me which held others at bay. Occasional remarks had substantiated the idea too. Late in 1944, the Government had decided to reduce the overseas service period for repatriation from five years right down to three years and eight months so I presume that decision was now responsible for Paddy's leaving. He looked rather miserable as he told me about it, or perhaps he was simply being serious for once. I discovered the true reason for his sad look within a few days.

I was on duty one day when the duty Sergeant approached me and hesitantly said: "I've come to ask you something." "Mm?" I asked. "I've got a ring. It's a good one," he stated rather blankly, which made me scrutinise his face, which I then saw was both pleading and apologetic. He knew then there was no other way but to come out with his message bluntly, so the well-built man with sleek, fair, wavy hair looked me straight in the eyes. "It's about Paddy. He wants to know if you'll accept this?" He was holding forth a ring in a case, an engagement type of ring.

The mystery was explained immediately. I'd suspected Paddy felt more than he said. He'd been a splendid companion; but I looked the Sergeant straight back in the eye, though I must also have looked thoughtful.

"Tell him I'm sorry," I said rather quietly.

He gave me a serious look then. "He's deadly serious y'know."

I didn't want to start a lot of explanations so I just shook my head and walked away. I could only think that Paddy had realised what my answer would be hence the messenger rather than himself. I saw Paddy again later. He had another try. He told me: "The one thing I'd like to do is to stay out here, to live here. If you'll stay with me I'll try for a position on a plantation. Come on, say you'll be a tea-planter's wife." It was no good. I knew there was something I'd have to sort out, but what it was I could not have told anyone. I promised to write to him, to his home in Belfast, and in a few days he was gone.

As soon as Paddy left I knew he'd been my protector. "Curly" lost no time in his hankering for me, but I was in no particular mood for anyone. Then one morning, soon after Paddy's departure, in my mail I found the strangest-looking envelope. It had been re-addressed three times. There was something vaguely familiar about the original handwriting on it, so that I could hardly contain my curiosity, and I ripped it open. Only one person, I thought, would have sent me this letter. A swarm of memories flooded back to me. The communication in my hand stirred strange feelings of a long past youth. I was now twenty-two, but I'd been just eighteen when I'd rather brutally finished the affair. Gordon had wanted me all to himself. I'd known him since I was sixteen. It had been one of those boy and girl affairs that go on and on unless something out of the ordinary happens, like moving home. But in our case war had happened. Oh no, it wasn't he who went to war and left me. I was the one who'd rushed off and he'd seemed mad at me for going, but we'd agreed to write one another.

On my first leave back home, I'd met him again but he was too serious about us and I didn't want that. I'd adjusted to a life of new things, new freedoms, and new ideas. I wondered why he didn't go away and join up like the others were doing. I'd just stopped writing after that, even though I'd earlier gone through a phase when I'd enjoyed keeping company with him. I'd been to his home on several occasions, and his cousin had commented on meeting me: "So, that's what makes you get dressed up every night." Then turning aside he threw me some sort of compliment.

The letter had been addressed to my former home, the one he knew at the time we'd been friendly. It was the new people there though who'd kindly forwarded it to the home my mother had moved to after my father's death, and she in turn had sent it on to me, through the coded address she knew would reach my secret abode.

151

I opened it to read a fairly short letter. It simply wondered if I might find time to write him once more. He told me he'd joined the Fleet Air Arm and a little of his life in it and nothing about hoping we might meet again. Then he apologised in case there were any spelling mistakes. It was such a pleasant letter. There was none of the heavy love stuff anymore. I realised that, like myself, he had found a new life too. I thought it would do no harm to write to a friendly sailor. I would simply tell him a little — as much as censorship of wartime letters would allow — of my life now in the Air Force. It would probably surprise him that I was now abroad somewhere, out of reach of home friends. I wrote quite soon to the code number that he'd shown on his letter telling him I was in Ceylon, wondering at the same time where he was stationed.

I received a reply so quickly I couldn't believe it was possible. And when I read his words I felt further stunned. He was stationed in Ceylon also and was joyful at the prospect of us meeting. Where was my camp? Could I meet him? Where? How soon? In Colombo?

Jennie was as surprised as I was, for she had known him too of course. He'd belonged to our dancing years. "Oh, you must go and meet him," she said, as if I was duty-bound to keep up with the past, for both our sakes.

I arranged to meet him and set off one day for Colombo on the Passion Wagon. I had on a fresh-looking, blue-checked dress, very fitting to the waist with a billowing skirt, a fashionable trend then. It accented a need to appear feminine as well as to show off bronzed limbs, as bothers the young and sometimes the old too. My hair still had its jungle look and was beginning to get quite long. It was a fairly windy day when I reached Colombo. We had arranged — for a now forgotten purpose — to meet outside a well known building. I had no idea where it was, so I found myself a rickshaw.

"Do you know where (I think it was called something like 'The White House') is?" I asked the brown skeleton that was beaming his good service over me.

"Oh, yes, lady. I take you there very quickly. In no time at all I will have you there." His lively brown eyes lied about his condition.

He set off at a pace, his fleshless hands gripping bars of wood so much more solid than they were. A quick steady trot took us, to my surprise, into the heart of the market area. We went further and further, deeper and deeper into a seething mass. I was surrounded by garments of all bright colours and shapes; I saw the dark red mouths of the men who constantly chewed betel, a mixture of leaves and nuts which contained a drug and made the chewers look as if they were bleeding to death from inside the mouth.

My runner had to slow down somewhat because of the crowds and I found myself being stared at from all sides. It was truly quite uncanny the feeling I got, of near fear. I felt a pure interloper among the seething Eastern mass of staring humanity. I almost began to pray that nothing would stop my driver from moving forward. I had a nasty suspicion, knowing the

153

dishonesty of Helen, that I might well be attacked and robbed, though in honesty I hadn't heard of it happening yet. Perhaps my nerves were over-stretched that day, and anyway I had little to be robbed of really.

I had little flesh to be robbed of either then, but I'm sure that day my body must have squeezed its last for when I took a hand across my brow as we got out of the market streets, I was extremely wet. I sat back and relaxed and for a while was happy to gaze with some astonishment at the supposed legs in front of me. My legs were sound in comparison with his, which were a composition of bones, sinews, veins, and skin only. He must have been at the job for many years. I learnt later, with no surprise, that those pullers died rather young and probably still do. A long time seemed to pass, then he suddenly pulled up, and with a sort of questioning look said: "Yes, lady. Where now lady?" I had the feeling we were both baffled with one another. He because I had not yet halted him. Me because I was wondering how on earth much further it could be.

I suddenly became startlingly aware that he had no idea where I wanted to be. I tried talking to him, but he just kept repeating: "Where lady wish to go?" In the end, fearful I'd get completely lost, I told him: "Take me back again," which he seemed to understand. And that is what he did, somewhat to my relief, though I knew by then that I was late for my appointment even in a slow-moving world.

It occurred to me later that he must have thought that I simply wanted a tour of interesting places. Back at base, I phoned the YMCA hopefully, and discovered

I'd been given up for that day, but Gordon was pleased to learn that I would now simply wait for him at the YWCA.

When we met, a veil of some sort lifted for me. I was gazing at a rather slim young man with sincere-looking eyes, and I thought at that moment a little shy of our meeting. It was in fact, in the eyes of youth, so long since we'd seen one another. I became aware of the same waving hair I remembered, which was peeping from the side of his naval cap covered in white for the tropics. He was glancing at me with a look that said time had not changed me. Beyond the looks I cannot remember what we said. I suppose we made conventional remarks at first.

We went and had tea somewhere, then he asked me to wait while he called in at the YMCA where he'd booked to stay. I sat on a leather settee in a large hall waiting for him. An old man, a native, was already seated there. I thought he must be some sort of hall porter perhaps, or someone trying to make a rupee from our boys.

Suddenly the old man turned to me. I glanced back at him, thinking he was about to tell me some rule of the club. Then I realised he just wanted to be friendly. A wonderfully wrinkled and deeply bronzed face also had the appearance of being wreathed in smiles, and the eyes had a light to them I'd only read about perhaps, or had I heard about such expressions in stories long ago. Stories I fancy in a long-ago Sunday school. Then the old man spoke: "I am a CHRISTIAN." He said it all with such slow emphasis.

All at once, the slightly ragged-looking creature with the face of God intent, was my master. It was so long since I'd given thought to my faith that I didn't know how to answer. But like a true Christian he did not seem to mind, did not even notice. My return smile, a little late in coming though, was all he had asked for really. His eyes turned from me again and rested somewhere he was fully expecting to go someday, or on someone he expected to meet, and quite soon I thought, for his smile was so radiant.

It seemed as if, because he knew he was in a building where the Christian white man moved about, then there also must be the God they claimed to know all about. I had almost refuted his idea with my silence, yet he never noticed. At that moment I felt ashamed that I had deliberately left behind my copy of the New Testament, as if I could control life without such things.

Gordon came bouncing back to me down some stairs, and said happily, "Let's go." I did not mention the old man, and I was also already aware that we were to go together from then on as if there had been no in between. Surely fate had planned it.

Outside, a great gust of wind caught us on the corner of a wide street and lifted my skirt completely over my head. I blushed beneath my tan when he said: "Oh, very nice." The sort of comment made by a young man with every intention of taking a friendship further, which is what he did.

By the end of the day I had agreed to spend a week's leave with him, and of course the only place to spend leave in Ceylon was up in the cool, cool hills. By then,

I was really ready for a break anyway, away from the heat. Six months without one had been much too long.

When I returned to camp that night, I told Jennie that Gordon had asked after her, and was looking forward to meeting her again too. "It's about time you two got together again," she commented. Her year's seniority over me always seemed to hold much wisdom, or perhaps that was the way I wanted it to appear at that moment.

There was still Eric in my life though. Had Jennie forgotten that or did she know me better than I knew myself? I began to hope they could get a replacement while I took a week's leave.

CHAPTER
SIXTEEN

As High as the Mountains

I was granted leave and joined some transport which would take me up into the hills, up to Nuwara Eliya. It was 6,000 feet up and we traversed roads that snaked across the hillsides, and, as so often in the tropics, the driving took a turn for the worse. I arrived there quite shattered and wondering how we had not tipped over the edge of every bend we took. But at the rest house I found Gordon already waiting for me. He'd arrived the previous night and spent it in the hotel lounge, on a settee, because it was full of officers. As he was just a petty officer they had been loath to give him a room. He jumped off a seat at my appearance, smiling broadly, almost with relief as if he had not expected me to turn up again. It was very refreshing to find myself in a climate not unlike an English summer, and for the first time in months I found I had to slip on a cardigan. The rest house had sufficient in comfort and chintzes to remind me of home and I had a most comfortable room. The staff echoed a long tradition of good service that added further to my comfort, and our first meal there boded well for the rest of our stay.

I'd taken my khaki slacks and battledress top, which was just as well because one of the memorable days of that week was when Gordon suggested we might try climbing Mount Pedro. We set off quite early and, although the climb was only two thousand feet, it put us eight thousand feet above sea level. It turned out to be an exhilarating climb that I could feel bringing roses back to my cheeks for a change. We raced each other on certain stretches and held hands on others, the excuse being I might tip down the mountain, which was quite steep.

At the top we stood for ages and admired the view as well as our own accomplishment, then Gordon sat me on top of the summit's monument which pronounced it was the top, and a snap was taken. It's still in my possession and shows me clutching my cardigan about me against the chill of the mountain's mist. The picture has faded a little by now of course and reached the condition where my children might fling it out when I die. That would be a pity because it was the moment of the turning point for me. We took other snaps too: Gordon by the lake, Gordon climbing a tree, myself having a nap on some grass. We'd watched as the native women picked tea in the fields, and visited a naval camp one night. We lived our week to the full and never thought to reveal the past, but even began to talk of things ahead as if we had to be together. Neither asked what happened but seemed to accept: it was some fault of youth that had caused us to part once before. We did not even wonder at such fate that had taken us so far across the world to meet again.

Yet I returned to camp with nothing definite in my thoughts except that I felt wonderfully refreshed with the break and was probably wondering when I would see Gordon again, but what should I write to Eric? And, equally important, what I should write to his family who kindly kept writing to me. I knew I was simply putting off the evil hour in a most cowardly fashion.

It was in June that the Government again reduced the repatriation period by yet a few more months and more men kept disappearing from our camp. And it was in June too that I realised that Irene was in love. I can't remember where she met Harry but I noticed the new light in her eyes, and I listened to her enthusiasm about art. Harry, you see, was an artist. And of course Ceylon was the perfect landscape. He showed her his drawings. She took regular recourse in telling me about them. I was pleased for her new-found happiness that I had known must come, and her delightful brown eyes took on a heavenly glow.

In the meantime, I had occasion to sharply repel one of the RAF Sergeants from his amorous advances. It came to a head one night, when he was in charge of a truck that was to take a crowd of us to some occasion. The truck was already fairly full when I arrived. Then, just as I was about to climb into its rear, "Determined" (I used to sometimes call him) waylaid me and physically pulled me to the front beside the driving compartment. In my embarrassment I hardly liked to

160

shout out my objections in front of a whole truck-load of girls, so I spent easily five minutes dissuading my amorous Sergeant with urgent whisperings, "No, no, no," I kept repeating. I didn't want to be wooed, or anything else he tried to suggest. It must have looked like shots from a silent movie as I stood there rejecting him while trying to remain a lady at the same time. In the end he released me and I crawled onto the form amidst muffled giggles and accusing "Ohs" and "Ahs", but, of course, the girls understood really. We were all prone to such advances where men are desperate for women. On reflection, I feel that we were a very able lot of WAAFs to come through such a time with so little damage to ourselves.

I always felt later that I had been very wise to take up with one young man in the first place, once I realised what the position was on camp, though Paddy was the loser perhaps one might admit. However, we did have good fun together, which is always nice to remember. Anyway, amidst pretend grumbles such as, "Hm, we were beginning to wonder how much longer you would hang on to him!" we got away at last, but it was not my last encounter with "Passion Boots". And by the time I left camp finally I had added a few more similes to my list of names about him. As we were jostled along the road to make up for a late start I commented: "I notice not one of you came to my rescue."

"Oh no," they laughed, "not likely; we waited to see which of you would win!" Of course they'd been peeping through the canvas.

While "pregnant" got larger each day and still remained on camp, one other girl had fallen in love and we heard delighted whispers that there was going to be a wedding, though duties were holding up the wedding date so far. It sounded very exciting for the camp. Pat was a lovely fair-haired girl who had managed to keep her peaches and cream complexion, though I couldn't remember her young man until Jennie handed me a photo recently. Yet in a way I had been more interested in their wedding than anyone else on camp, which you will see why later.

As time passed, we all came to love Ceylon more and more, in spite of our encounters with its vile creatures. Such as the day I was chased up and down our hut by what looked like a wasp which had been on special calories to make it grow so large. In the end it tired me out first and I only escaped by a shattering jump onto my bed and by dragging my net about me. Then I sat and grinned as it took umbrage at me through the net before flying off. The girls were laughing, calling me things like "Rotten Meat" as I wondered why I hadn't thought of the net earlier. Screams often ricocheted through a hut as an unexpected insect began an attack on one of us. In the end we had learnt to laugh at that part of our existence. It was the heat though, that never seemed to stop taking its toll of us, and because of that we began to get visions of home, and I think, began to wonder if we'd ever return there again.

It was in July that my next surprise happened. This time it was in the form of a telegram. They were quite commonplace to receive at home in those days, and regrettably often proclaiming very sad news, such as when my father had died. Whatever was in one sent all the way to me in Ceylon? When I opened it though, I saw it was not from home at all. The message read: "Repatriated. Will you marry me?" It was signed "Gordon".

From that moment, the world took a great big heaving dizzy turn, for the next few weeks anyway. My answer this time was "yes". The girl I'd had the discussion with about men and marriage was astonished. How could I, within a few weeks, change my mind so irrevocably? I showed her his photograph. "Yes," she said, "he has rather special eyes." But I could understand her admonishment of me. I was even taken aback myself. Yet Jennie did not seem in the least surprised and at once wanted to know where and when and all the rest that goes with weddings. Irene only looked thoughtful about it, and I think spoke the minimum of words, though she was more in love with Harry too.

The news quickly spread amongst the small WAAF community, and they all seemed to want to come and see the wedding. I sometimes wonder what happened to that important telegram. I've wished many times that I'd hung onto it. Not many girls have the written evidence that it really was the man who did the proposing. On the other hand I have often been able to blame the heat for making me jump so recklessly into marriage too. The telegram must have got lost in the rush that followed.

First of all I went and advised our officer what I intended doing, and then I hit my first stumbling block. It was so doing that I discovered how serious she was in her mother image towards us, sheltering us from all the harms which such a place offered. It showed too on her youngish face as she told me with deadly seriousness: "Well then, we must see about this. First of all I want you to send a telegram home to your parents and ask their permission."

I must have blinked at her in disbelief because she then added something about being responsible for all of us girls, and I could see that there was no moving her, so I sent a telegram: "Please grant permission for me to marry Gordon." I felt a fool sending it, and my mother must have thought the heat was melting my brain, because the last thing I'd ever done was to ask my parents' permission from the moment I'd made up my mind to join the Air Force, and often before that. But, of course, the officer had a good point, which I see now.

I got the briefest reply: "Permission granted — Congratulations." I was quite sure of course that she must have been feeling upset too that I'd let Eric down. She had liked him a lot, and she had never met Gordon, though my father had briefly. In fact I learned much later she had got rather a shock at receiving a telegram of any sort, thinking I'd been hurt or worse.

However, the telegram was followed by a very beautifully bound prayer book. The accompanying note thought I might like to carry one during the service. I felt it was my mother's way of saying, "Are you sure about this?"

I thought that the officer smiled happily for me when I showed her the reply. I feel sure now that I should have invited her to the wedding too. It never occurred to me at the time. Officers were a class we must not interfere with, I'd been led to believe.

It was arranged that I meet Gordon in Colombo, because we had to apply at the Registry Office there for a special licence to marry. Gordon hugged me when I arrived. He was wearing white slacks and a navy jacket and I'd never seen such an eager face as he practically raced me towards a dark-coloured taxi, then gave the driver some instructions.

We'd only been travelling a minute when a second taxi slewed across the road from the right and we had a sideways, head-on crash. It was my second one that day. The bus I'd travelled up on had gone at such a speed, it had caught a village native carrying two pails on a yoke across his shoulders. The sort of thing that happened in fiction in The Keystone Cops and we'd left him spinning round, though he seemed unharmed. Almost immediately, natives appeared from everywhere. The two drivers jumped out and a great slanging match started between them, with others in the crowd taking sides also. Gordon opened his door, grabbed me by the arm and pulled me out, and literally forced his way through the crowd. We took a rickshaw each after that and left the gabble of high-pitched voices screaming behind us.

When we arrived, the Registry Office held only three people. A man was dressed in European clothes, but his colours did not match. The suit did not fit, and a loose

165

white collar with a creased and badly knotted tie hung a few sizes too big. He was standing at the counter with a woman on either side of him, each in a sari. They appeared to have to repeat some words after the clerk behind the counter, and we felt sure that the man must be marrying one of the women with the other as witness perhaps. They had the look of three about to be slaughtered, and were obviously poor people. The clerk also took their fingerprints, which made us assume no one could write.

We registered ourselves, and I arranged through my camp Padre that the service should take place at All Saints Church in Galle, the same one where Pat had wanted us to have a double wedding. We would have been delighted to do so but Gordon was unable to get that time off, and Pat's wedding had to go ahead before we could get registered. I think she was almost on the point of postponing hers until our date but her husband-to-be couldn't change dates either. That was a great pity. We bought my ring in Colombo. While the shopkeeper had coffee brought to us on a tray we chose. But only one ring fitted me, a plain 22ct one, so we took it. Jennie set to arranging the guests, while I was about to decide what to wear, when Irene stepped in. She'd just had a very nice blue dress made up from material sent from home. It was in Moygashel and the rever collar and three-quarter sleeves were pleasantly scalloped, and luckily I'd always suited blue. Irene and I being the same size, it fitted perfectly. Jennie was to be my bridesmaid and she borrowed a white dress with a pattern on it. I bought blue veiling from a market stall in Galle and made a hat, and Kathleen made one in white for Jennie. Irene unfortunately had to stay on duty, which was just as well really since I'd borrowed her best dress of course.

Gordon arrived at Koggala the day before the wedding, and it still remains a mystery to me how Passion Boots became our best man, for I felt sure Jennie knew about him. Also to make me think, was the fact that the Sergeant who'd offered me the ring on Paddy's behalf, had now offered to give me away. His name was Harold Albert Leslie Miller, commonly known as "Dusty".

I was secretly hoping he would not give away that little episode of my recent past. I don't know if he did but there must have been a splendid opportunity when a bachelor party was held for Gordon on our camp. One very tiny episode though was revealed on the same day that Gordon arrived. Mr McCready had apparently heard about my wedding and Gordon's arrival at camp, so he sent an invitation for us to sit with him that day and share a drink. We accepted it and went and settled ourselves on his veranda. Then to my great embarrassment he immediately told us: "Oh dear, oh dear. You've absolutely shattered Thomas. He kept telling me all these months, you were the girl he would marry. You've quite broken his heart. I don't know how to console him." Thomas was the young Irishman who had rescued me from the first and final dance on camp after our arrival. But apart from waving to him whenever I saw him, I'd had nothing further to do with him. It seems true what they say — "Faint heart never won fair maiden". Mr McCready however, wished us well, and perhaps he had been looking for an invitation, but that never came to mind either. I've wondered since if he kept a diary of events on camp. It would have made both sad and exciting reading for everyone. So many lights of love trying to burn for each WAAF. As some of you might think — What a War!

On the morning of my wedding I woke early as usual. I lay and watched as an early twilight gradually broke into the miraculous dawn we were used to. A veil of gold shimmered over everything. Behind the veil the creatures about us had already scurried away after their night's activities. Suddenly the veil melted and the unrelenting sun took up its position. Irene was awake also, so we went for a swim. I'd half hoped to see Gordon at the water too, even though it was said to be unlucky to see one another before the wedding, but those things only happened back home. Anyway, he didn't arrive.

I returned to the hut, washed my hair and wrapped it in pipe cleaners to give it some curl. When it came to combing it out later, I knew I'd nervously wrapped it too tight, and my already thick hair just looked a frizzy mess. I combed it and combed it to tame it more, worrying about what it would look like at the altar.

The transport was to take me to Galle at eleven o'clock, along with the other WAAFs who could get off duty. It alarmed me, though only slightly, to discover the same truck was to pick up Gordon, who'd been given one of the men's huts for the night. However, again I threw stupid superstition aside and realised we were very lucky to be allowed camp transport at all.

We made the stop for him further along the road, but the driver returned looking a bit perturbed. The bachelor party had been such a success it seemed, that every damned man had neglected to ensure that Gordon would be awakened in time for his wedding. He was still sleeping off the effects of it when they rapped on his door and I had been worrying about how my hair would look!

A howl of sympathy went up from everybody on the truck. They all helped me to make light of it but I was already feeling nervous, having last minute misgivings, and didn't know who I should be blaming for the hold-up, while pretending to stay calm. Gordon must have broken every record for a Bridegroom preparing for their wedding. We heard his feet racing before he leapt into the seat beside the driver. His profile affirmed the good time the boys had given him; how they'd taken the Navy to the bosom of their Royal Air Force hearts — the stinkers!

I recently told someone I got married on a Friday, which they thought was a very strange day to marry on. For us though then, the war had taken the weekends out of weeks, made one day just like another, and I don't think weekends ever became the same again afterwards.

Once in church Dusty walked me to the altar, where Mr. Jourdain, a serious-looking man, tall and thin with brown hair, gave Gordon and me a ministerial talk about the seriousness of marriage before he started the

169

service. It seemed to send us both into spasms of great fear, for I was aware how much we were both trembling as we knelt. My fingers were convulsively gripping my prayer book. I hadn't really had time to give much thought to the question of marriage myself, and the minister's words seemed frighteningly late. A wedding is a corruption of the nervous system for the good and conscientious, I have often thought since.

It was as well I had not got the bouquet I ordered, I would have quivered it free of petals. In fact I had ordered one for an original date we hoped to have the wedding, but it had to be altered and I am ashamed to say the florist would be left with a bouquet on his hands. It is one of the bits of guilt that has remained with me, but in this instance it was a case of *C'est la guerre* rather than *C'est la vie*.

We had a wedding group picture taken by a Galle photographer who managed to get a wide drainpipe on the church wall in an imposing position between myself and Passion Boots, and I noticed Pat also has a similar drainpipe, though on a different wall.

Afterwards, everyone at church came, and we had an English-type lunch served in the nearby "New Oriental" hotel. Then we celebrated with drinks that Gordon had ordered from the Sergeant's mess. He also remembers the Padre saying to him: "I shouldn't have any more to drink. It's your wedding day remember!" Whereupon Gordon felt mortally wounded, because at the time he hadn't had a drop of anything, but the Padre himself seemed quite merry. Then there was half an hour of panic when we discovered one of the girls

170

had somehow gone missing. However, it turned out that she had been curious to go and see the historical bits of Galle and hadn't thought to mention it. Someone found her by the harbour. We all had a terrible fear she had been kidnapped or something equally bad. Jennie, who'd done all the arranging, was truly churning at the stomach with worry until she was found.

I suffered another difficult moment on the evening after the wedding. We'd arranged to go to a dance to further the celebrations, and one of the Americans from the camp along the road, with whom I'd already had a tussle, asked me to dance — a persistent type. He immediately began to get himself into a very close hustle with me. His neck wrapped itself across mine and he took on a dreamy slouch. Sweet insincere nothings began to pour from him until I felt obliged to tell him that I had a partner with me.

"A par-dner?" he questioned.

"Yes," I offered, "it's my husband in fact."

He straightened himself from his amorous leanings as if a whole regiment of US generals had suddenly appeared and he never asked for a dance again after that. But a wedding ring, I discovered later, was still no deterrent to some. Maybe the hubby, but not the ring. Apart from that my heart was as high as the mountains.

Our honeymoon consisted of one brief night. It was spent in a room of the house of the bank manager of Galle. He was a middle-aged Englishman called Mr Benson, who'd also heard about the wedding, and had most kindly invited us to share his home for the night.

It was the bride on this occasion that had to leap from bed very early and go to work next morning. I had to be on duty at 8 o'clock. Gordon came to camp with me and later came to chat with me through my window space, but he had to leave that day. It was to be many, many nights before we had a real honeymoon.

CHAPTER
SEVENTEEN

Irene Makes a Decision

Although Gordon was due for repatriation, like many others, he simply hung around waiting for a ship, sometimes doing light duties. About a week after our wedding, I was on duty when I was asked to report to a RAF officer. I was puzzled. In fact, I had never set eyes on a signals' officer. I could not imagine why he wanted me. I'd never had trouble about my work, and was working as conscientiously as ever. The officer was seated, but turned as I entered his office: "I hear you've just been married and that you didn't have a honeymoon."

"Er, well — er — yes, that's right" I stammered in surprise.

"Well, you're to have one. I'll arrange for someone to take over. I'm sorry I didn't know about it sooner."

I was so taken aback I'm sure I forgot to thank him, or perhaps I did. It worried me though that Jennie and Irene might have to put in extra hours. I hoped he meant what he said about making arrangements. Yet I was pleased to be allowed away to at least see Gordon. I sent a message to say I'd meet him in Colombo first, as I wanted to buy something.

\When I got to Colombo, it was to discover that Gordon was having a turn in hospital now, and all I could do was to book into the YWCA and visit him there. I felt I should have gone back to camp, but I felt embarrassed at the thought of having to explain away no honeymoon once again, though now I don't know why.

I was seated on the veranda of the YWCA one afternoon, reading a magazine over a pot of tea, a novelty for someone who'd been stuck in the jungle for seven months without any reading matter at all, except that on notice boards. A young man came towards me and spoke. He asked me if I could tell him how to get to a certain building. He was brisk of manner and an officer type I thought. I couldn't help him, and he seemed in a bit of a quandary about some things, so I listened to his fed-up mood. I decided to ask him to join me in afternoon tea, and this seemed to cheer him up. He pulled up a chair at once, full of thanks, and helped himself to sandwiches and cake with the tea I poured for him. As soon as he'd finished, he excused himself, having decided to continue his search but before he left he looked and said: "Do you fancy going to the cinema this evening?"

Being alone and fed-up myself, I accepted. I'd never been to a Ceylon cinema yet. He called for me later, and we went to a one-storey building in the city. I've forgotten now what film we saw, so it couldn't have been a memorable one, but one thing we saw I will never forget. It haunted me for many weeks, and I can see it clearly in detail to this day, and it still makes me grimace. It was indeed memorable.

I don't know what I expected in a cinema in Ceylon, but they were very similar to our own really, and that night I discovered they used our newsreels too. As soon as the news began I brightened at the thought. At Koggala we heard nothing, which was probably why the camp news had such an impact on us. We were rather like people who cling to their village and learn nothing of the outside world.

That night as the stranger and I watched, I grew more and more horrified at the sights I saw. They were showing a lengthy reel of the pictures taken in the German concentration camps after the victory in Europe. I cringed in my velvet seat at the sight of great heaps of near skeletons, and then of barely moving but walking skeletons, who nevertheless were trying to smile. I was appalled. What sort of world were we in! Who had done this? The hundreds seated about me were horrified too, I knew, for the silence alone reflected their horror, and because they were all black, I felt almost guilty that I belonged to the white races. Did they not, I wondered, imagine we all had such a streak?

It was with a serious grasp of the hand that the stranger and I parted that night, without even trying to convey our feelings about the horror to one another. What could anyone say! I felt I'd grown years older in minutes. Well at least the Sinhalese would understand why we were stalking around their island in an interloping fashion now, I thought.

175

I'm quite sure that because of the peace of our existence in such a lovely land, the sudden visual shock had been much greater to me there, though that is difficult to prove. Such a massacre would have looked devastating anywhere. I didn't sleep comfortably that night.

Gordon was released from hospital the day before I had to return to Koggala. In the evening we went out to take a stroll around Colombo, and to see if there were stars for us above. Walking along one charming wide road I realised Gordon must still be feeling below par when he commented: "It's a pity there aren't any seats to sit on." He was right, because the evenings are so beautiful just sitting beneath the heavens was sheer delight.

"Come on," he said, "let's have a rest here."

We were at the rear of what seemed to be quite large houses, and many were simply edged at the end of the gardens with a few pretty shrubs. "Yes," I said, "good idea," and we plonked ourselves on the grass in the exclusive quiet of the road.

We sat between two shrubs, being neither in nor out of the garden. We began to talk, but we'd hardly spoken a few words when a sharp voice as well as a figure appeared behind us. We turned in fright to see a fully dressed soldier with a long rifle cocked towards us. "Who goes there?" he yelled at us.

We shot to our feet. "Sorry," said Gordon, "but we were just sitting having a rest for a minute. We didn't realise . . ." But the confronter wouldn't allow him to continue. "This is the residence of . . .

We were both so shocked, the highly important man's name slipped from our brains; indeed I don't remember it ever getting into mine. But the man's title must have been something like, "His Excellency The Governor of Ceylon", and perhaps was. Why else armed soldiers guarding it?

The soldier began by being adamant that we should follow him into the building. We felt like spies, the manner he was taking with us. Then my feminine wile took a turn for genius, though I think our desperation proved its birth. "Look," I pleaded, "we've only just been married. We haven't even had the chance to see each other." I felt I was speaking the truth anyway. "That's right," Gordon agreed, sorry he hadn't thought of it first and added: "We'd no idea where we were."

Then astonishingly, the soldier lowered his weapon, and said, "Oh, all right, go along". We'd discovered that the Sinhalese do have hearts, despite their righteous attitude.

We thanked him, appreciating him for his humanity before we split the distance between the rotten building and us. Why, we asked ourselves later, did it not have a more solid barrier about it if it was so important. However, an armed soldier had been enough to frighten the life out of us. When the shock had passed though, we managed to laugh. To think that of all the many houses in Colombo, we had to pick the wrong one. It was like finding the needle in the haystack at last, and the results just as sharp.

I returned to camp full of the intention now of applying for a home posting, because Gordon had managed to tell me after all that they expected to be on the move soon.

When I mentioned this to Irene, she turned to me immediately and said: "If you're going back, then I'm coming too. We should be able to travel home together."

Again it sounded simple and we both made our application to Mother Superior, for that's how I'd begun to think of her. Soon afterwards though, she sent once more that she'd like to see me.

I crossed to the Admin hut to find her. "You're a very close friend of Irene, aren't you?" she asked as soon as I appeared.

I was bound to look puzzled, and answered: "Yes, I am."

"Is it correct then that she's married?" she said, drawing her brows together in question.

"Yes, that's right, she is." And I felt something else was coming.

"I see. I didn't realise it. D'you know why she's applied for a home posting, then?"

"I think so. She has a marriage problem, and I think she wants to get back to sort it out."

"I see. Thank you. Right'o, that's all." But I left her with a frown still.

In fact, Irene had told me that Harry wanted to marry her. She'd told him her story, and now she was ready to go and clear up the mess. And I was glad she seemed to have found the strength to go ahead and make a new life.

It was only two or three days after that, that the greatest news of all came. Our war, the war in Japan, or more correctly for us, Burma, was over now too. The atom bomb had been the final straw for the Japs. Now it was time for everyone out East to celebrate, just as they'd done for VE day in Britain and Europe.

The surrender took place on August 14th 1945, just three and a half weeks after my wedding, a lovely extra present. Now, we all thought, everybody can relax and go home. There'd be no more fighting for our men. By then Gordon was already on his way back.

I knew then that it would be safe, from the war point of view, to write and tell Eric the truth. I had always had a terrible fear that if he got killed, I would have been left with some guilt had I written earlier and told him the truth of my feelings. I did it somehow, though it was a miserable deed for me. I wrote a lengthy letter, trying to excuse myself, praying he would understand, yet I knew in my heart that he wouldn't. It was an afternoon that I felt something in the New Testament might have helped me. It turned out to be far from the last word between us.

I was on night duty when VJ — victory against Japan, was put through to us. I'd lain down for a short rest at about 2 a.m., under a net in a room next to our small teleprinter one, with the satisfaction of knowing one of the radio bods would wake me if a message started.

Another bod came though, not from radio ops, and said: "Come on, up you get. We're all celebrating. It's Victory." Assuring myself that someone would send for me still, I joined about two dozen people in our building. It was clear they had already got a head start on me, though they began to make sure I would catch up with the celebrating. I was no drinker and never had been, but that night there was just no refusing. And anyway, the mood was already very infectious between everybody. And so, they poured me a beer too. After about an hour when the glass in my hand had been constantly kept topped up, a thought occurred to me. I was feeling rather swimmy, my eyes felt bright, my cheeks well flushed, yet I was still bolt upright on a wooden chair. It was a long time since I'd sat regularly on a real chair, apart from at the YWCA, and I began to think that the idea of sitting struck me as rather foolish and somewhat unnatural to me now. I looked at two or three more who were sitting, and suddenly felt inclined to giggle. And what a strange feeling chairs had now. Was it really so long since we'd had chairs. Yes, it was, I told myself. Mine felt hard and uncomfortable now, even difficult to balance on without any arms to it. I hadn't even realised some people on camp had chairs. I betted to myself it was the officers. My seat had had to get used to beds and sand only.

Everybody was singing like mad, as if each had won the war all by themselves, and a few girls too. I recognised one or two of them through the mist, but who was that man sitting on a chair like mine? He wasn't singing. All of a sudden I drew a deep breath. My God, I told myself, it's the Padre. Whatever must he be thinking of the scene before him I wondered? He seemed to be the only one behind his glasses not smiling, not flushed, not bawling his head off. God seemed to have given him amazing powers, for he seemed to be drinking as much as the next man.

I really can't remember what happened after that very much. It got a little more blurred as the minutes passed. I was delightfully, ridiculously under the drink (not drunk — they fall about) and I just sat singing and trying not to giggle. I just couldn't keep a straight face, whatever that is called. Half-drunk I suppose.

I had left my home in 1941, a mere child really of eighteen years, and an innocent lamb they'd wrapped in a label of blue. It was now 1945. It had taken me four years to get merrily drunk for the first time. And I cannot remember having any dreadful after-effects such as had been described by various other WAAFs, during my epic of the last years. It had always been the after-effects which made them vow, "Never again".

Shortly after victory both Irene and I entered hospital again, then after that we both got orders to pack up. In one respect I now wanted to get back home, yet it was with an emotional pull that I packed to leave the spot that had become home in every sense of the word to a small band of happy girls. It had become our own very exclusive world, where we'd reigned almost as queens. Strangely, though I've forgotten some of the names, and we were all first names there, the faces are still fairly clear. Even the shapes of some bodies are still familiar, for as I've told you we seldom wore clothes, and shoulder lines in particular come to mind.

I was tempted before I started the story to try and contact each one of the crowd. Put an advert. in *The*

181

Times and elsewhere, but after some thought I knew it would be just trying to take the sun from the sky. I think we might prefer to remember ourselves just as we were, a happy young bunch that world events had unconsciously thrown together. Yet I am sure that each WAAF of Koggala could also fill many pages about all the excitement we had thrust upon us. Truth of that statement came to me many years later out of the blue one afternoon.

I'd written a short article as my contribution to a series called, *What Did You Do In The War, Mummy?* for my local paper. It was a brief statement of our life at Koggala, but it got placed in heavy type. I got inundated with questions later, as did Jennie, who I'd mentioned too, and who was at the time working in a hospital. "The patients were fascinated," she said. But it was two days after the article appeared that my phone rang, so I answered. I heard a male voice saying: "I saw your story in the paper. Would you mind telling me if it was Koggala you were stationed at?"

"Yes, it was," I assured him, my heart beginning to flutter at a voice who knew of it.

"I thought so. There was only one jungle station. I was there too."

We talked for at least an hour. Every breath of that long-past adventure was turned over and over in our minds, and with words. I knew then that I had not been wrong in thinking Koggala was something unique. His enthusiasm too kept us trapped with each other as we relived those vital days.

182

He mentioned one name in particular to me. Of course I remembered her, I told him. But he did not enlarge on their relationship. She was fair, curvaceous, always laughing like the rest of us. I knew I was getting a good sniff at one war secret that can never be revealed. He did not tell me his name, and I knew there would be no point in asking it.

He remembered it all as if it was yesterday, the bay, the planes, the smuggling, and how Jennie had us all in a panic the day she fell over the wrong side of the reef into shark-infested waters. Our memories tumbled forth just as an old record is played, with sincere gratitude for its existence. We longed to talk forever, to bring back our youth. Koggala had been a kind of dream.

But it was away from that same dreamy world that Irene and I had to turn. I carefully packed the garnet necklace Gordon had given me as a wedding gift, I didn't want to lose that, and the green Parker Pen Irene had somehow secretly managed to get for my twenty-second birthday. The rest I stuffed in hard, for I'd bought quite a number of things. I also carefully wrapped the three wooden elephants that formed the stand for a nut-bowl, and the two elephant bookends, gifts from the girls for my wedding.

We were sad to leave Jennie but in fact it was not long before everyone was on the move, and she flew to Singapore and Hong Kong as a prelude to repatriation. I don't think I could have borne to watch the tearing apart of the camp, and sadly I know that a hotel, called in fact "Koggala Hotel" now stands there where *our* huts were, and strangers must bathe in *our* bay, watch *our* sunsets. Tourists, who have no conception of the worth of the ground beneath their feet.

Irene and I travelled to the airport, almost passing out with the task of so much to carry. And then for the first time in our lives we climbed aboard an aircraft. It was something I'd longed to do for four years, but had never been offered the chance. If an aircraft can be termed "rickety", ours was. Inside it had a pattern of long and short wooden seats, and we were asked to sit still as much as possible, though I couldn't imagine what else we could do. It was a terrific thrill though as we soared easily upwards. Not long after we'd started the journey, another WAAF also sitting next to me, without apology but looking pale, lay herself across my knees just as the one on the ship had done. I spent most of the long, hot and uncomfortable trip feeling sorry for her.

We were on our way to India. It had been a dream only, for years, that I should one day be able to see the land where my father had spent much of his service. But I'd never have believed that time would ever arrive. Yet here I was on the very brink of experiencing some of the wonders my ears had been filled with as a growing girl. Perhaps, in some silent way, he would be there in India to greet me, in spirit or love.

Irene was excited too, to be passing through it, or at least touching it on our way home, for, as usual, we were not really sure where we were going exactly.

India though, was going to be more of an adventure than either of us could have suspected. We were on the verge of a vital period in British history, and Irene and I were to become, in a way, two of its victims.

CHAPTER
EIGHTEEN

Penniless and Hotter than Hell

It was early evening when we sighted India. We'd started off about 9 a.m. and the flight had been long and exhausting. It was a blessed relief to see a long curving line of the Indian coast and to be told we'd be landing shortly.

We dropped down to Bombay Airport and, despite our weariness, fell eagerly onto the tarmac. We were led across to a terminal building and our first true sight of the country almost made us gasp. Only good manners prevented it. He was a black-skinned male, taller than my ignorance had expected of Indians, and he was clothed completely in pure gold lamé. He smiled and flashed his pure white teeth in greeting to us, then his turbaned head bowed slightly. The turban too was all gold and wonderfully wrapped, and matched his breeches and longish jacket. His lower legs were wrapped in golden puttees and then there were soft golden slippers.

In one instant all the magical stories of the romantic east were standing there before me. I knew at once that

186

I was going to enjoy passing through India, as I'd never enjoyed anything before. My father had been right: "There's nowhere else like it," he'd said. He'd spent a number of his bachelor years there. That indeed must have been storytelling, considering what I've since read about our men in the ruby of the Empire in those halcyon days for them. How well men provide for their needs!

We took a train, an exceedingly civilised one this time, in contrast to those we'd occasionally used in Ceylon, for they had looked more like a great moving caterpillar sprouting humans from all sides. It was nearer to an English mode of travel than anything we'd tried up until then, as we travelled towards Bombay City.

I found myself seated against a very blonde-haired, pink-complexioned man. He gave Irene and me a quick look of interest then turned rather quickly away. He had a paperback book in his hand and seemed to go on reading again. A few stops later he picked up some bags and prepared to leave, then quite shyly he turned to me and said: "Would you like this?"

He was already placing the book in my lap. I gave him a quick shy smile myself and said "Thanks". He looked typical of an Englishman who'd been out there too long and did not know how to continue his interest with conversation. A businessman perhaps, I thought, living a bachelor existence without the availability of the usual perks laid on for the troops. Perhaps he'd heard of our low pay and the book was his commiseration, or perhaps he just had a kind and lonely heart.

We found our way to our hotel. It appeared in the heart of the city, was called The Astoria, and had been taken over especially for us and our kind. Like the train, it seemed splendidly civilised after the jungle, was extremely clean, and we were soon embedded in a room with two others, and were able to look out from very large apertures onto a particularly busy street.

It became clear very early that we were there for an indefinite period, which rather took us aback. Some of the others told us: "Oh, we've been waiting weeks. We can't see you getting away any sooner."

Aha, we thought, but we are returning on compassionate grounds in a sense. It was now my turn as one of the "marrieds" to gain privilege over others, I imagined. And that is what Irene and I told ourselves later out of their hearing. We were fluffing up our wool again.

It might sound like a dream for any of you hearing this that all we had to do from then on was to go about and enjoy ourselves. Some day a ship would be found that might take us home to England. In actual fact, dreams come to a standstill when pockets are empty, and that is exactly the position we found ourselves in for many weeks ahead. We could not even afford a stamp to post a letter. Yet in a sense we did make some of the dream reality, though we had to use some slightly devious methods, out of line with our character.

We did not know it then, but in actual fact the position we were in was this: the war was at an end

188

truly, but a lot of tidying up had to be done, and sometimes the aftermath is as bad as the war. We had given plenty of service to entitle us to be repatriated on the length of that alone, but there were far greater priorities than ours. These were the weak and the wounded and in some cases the seriously ill, the men who had been on the Burma front. They, quite rightly, took precedence in the queue for ships, though as many as possible of them were flown home. Many thousands were longing to get there. Whole nations had become like a giant pack of cards each with its members scattered, shuffled about right across the globe. We were just a tiny trump in the bellow to go home, though to us our rights seemed important.

The joker though, was the poverty trap we found ourselves in, and was simply due to the matter of too usual procedures. As we were documented as being on our way home, that is where the papers, pay and otherwise had been sent, to be ready and waiting for our arrival there. It was a bit of a disaster, but there was nothing to do but put up with the effects of it.

At first, of course, we did have some rupees in our purse, but with so much time on our hands, so many new things to see, they soon went into tills. Had we been immediately by a beach as we were at Koggala, we could have spent many hours swimming. It would have been a blessed relief to do so as India was akin to jumping from the frying pan into the flames. There were no sea breezes playing around us as they had in Ceylon most of the time. Walking in Bombay was like walking in an oven.

189

Our first adventure was simply to walk about and stare. We pushed through colourful crowds along pavements, and often came to a spot where we almost had to step across the most appalling sights of humanity. Beggars were everywhere. They had twisted arms, strange looking eyes, fleshless limbs, and a dirty rag about the groin and sometimes a dull turban slung around the head. At times every bit of the body was revealed, as they lay sprawled in sleep or stupor across a pavement at our feet. A strange contrast to the dream at the airport.

A further contrast was to actually see the rich too. In the entire world, women could not be more elegant than many that we saw crossing roads in Bombay. The wonderful saris they floated along in rivalled even the glory of the fantastic sunsets, the miraculous dawns. Humanity in Bombay was God and the Devil quietly tearing at each other's throats with the Devil having the upper hand. How else could such beauty walk about so unaware? A stranger from the world could only turn a blind eye to suffer it, before beginning to wonder why.

It was sickening too to gaze at monuments to our own royalty, who were Emperors of India then, too and read inscriptions of their worth beneath monstrous bronzes. The words were meant to inspire not love, but fear and adoration. One felt almost that one should not pass without kneeling to them.

The requirement for drinks, of any sort, was always a priority in the grinding heat, and took Irene and me into cafés. There, we would be pounced upon, though most politely of course, by any white men around.

Usually they would invite us to join them for a drink. This meant coffee often, which was wonderfully black and deliciously flavoured. Or, often, a cooling lime was favoured by all. Next they might suggest a ride around to see the sights. The men, generally speaking, were just seeking feminine companionship. We were particularly aware on those occasions of a very high standard of manners among them, though whether this was to impress the natives or us was hard to tell. However, I think most of us were careful of our behaviour in a foreign land.

It was when we entered a café for the first time that we caught the advantage of so doing. It was a sort of raised dais with low walls, and we seated ourselves at a bamboo table. In a minute the waiter arrived as we talked, but before we could order, he spoke to us of a request from a nearby table to accept a drink from its occupants. It was exactly the way we'd seen people do in films, so Irene and I lost no time in behaving like stars. We told the waiter: "Tell the gentlemen that is very kind. We'll take a coffee."

The message of course was their cue to rise and join us with a delighted smile. It was not only civilised, but also very advantageous to two girls gasping for treats, due simply to being penniless. We couldn't believe our luck and how easily it worked. I've since come to the conclusion that at least seventy-five percent of female babies should be done in at birth, then the remainder would be treated like queens. The set-up out East in those days proved it. A shortage will create a demand, and a high price will be offered for it. In fact, I've heard

191

of a jungle tribe where the women do this regularly, and lie about being waited on through life.

However, there were plenty of days of course when no such luck occurred, and as time passed we really became absolutely less than paupers. The WAAF Officer helped out once by a minute loan, but it was like soothing a hungry elephant with a chocolate drop. Then one day a miracle happened. Irene opened a letter from home and out of it dropped two whole pounds in the form of a postal order. We felt we should look for a church and go and bless her mother. But we had many hours to fill, and again we became destitute, and seriously thought of lining up with the city's beggars along the pavements. We almost squealed with derision when an outstretched hand begged from us, which they did truly.

We had only a few annas left one day between us and, gasping as always with thirst, we risked going into a cheap-looking café, where we hoped the prices were rock bottom. Inside it was small and absolutely full of native men. We remembered what the officer told us about behaving like the masters and we strolled across to the one empty table and ordered coffee. The whole clientele began staring at us as if we were from another planet, but we kept our cool and the drinks arrived. Halfway through them though, we began to feel alarmed. What if we hadn't enough to pay? At second glance the other customers didn't look so poor after all. What, we wondered, did the Indians who owned cafés do with people who couldn't pay? Would we be sent to the Black Hole of Calcutta?

As so often in such circumstances, the ridiculous takes over, and we began to giggle. This elevated us to a more extreme planet in all the interested brown eyes. Perhaps their women did not giggle, we began to think.

"You ask for the bill," I pleaded of Irene, who always giggled more effectively than me.

It was like the grace of every angel descending when the waiter gave us our slip, and we gathered together enough, though we had only one anna left. We were really in such a sweat we decided not to risk so much again, as well as so little.

Whether white males got rarer I cannot recall, but we reached desperation point for money. Then Irene had a real brainwave. "I know; I'll try and sell one of Harry's drawings."

I had visions of us searching around Bombay for three brass balls, but I gave her a comforting look, because the suggestion gave me that sort of feeling anyway. My timing was bad though, because immediately she'd made the suggestion she began to waver. How would Harry take it? Was it really fair? He'd asked her to take some of them back so that he could complete some more. They were mostly only pen and pencil drawings, and mainly of Sinhalese ladies, but they were very good as far as my art knowledge extended. I could only draw a triangle. It took just a tiny further consideration to determine that Harry would have to develop a humanitarian streak if he ever got to know.

"Tell him you lost some," I suggested. With all the luggage we had I felt it was a most reasonable explanation, if the time ever came, and perhaps Harry had a bad memory anyway, like most men. He might not miss just one. We walked about the city's shops, armed with a carefully rolled-up drawing, until we spotted a large bookshop that also had a display of drawings and pictures of varying grades, so, grasping the robes of the Empire about us we entered.

Inside it was almost empty. A male assistant in a white jacket and long white comboy approached. He had almost reached us, had, in fact, given us a nod, when he was halted by a rather imperious voice. Leaving Irene with words about to tumble, he hesitated, but then turned away from us, and with a further summons went across to an elegant Indian pair, who could have been man and wife, and left us standing. It had been the woman's voice who'd summoned him.

As soon as he reached the couple, the woman gesticulated and laughed quite volubly, and a distinct impression crept over both Irene and me, that it was her intention to let us know that, as far as they were concerned, British Imperialism was dead.

The assistant dealt with the couple by beckoning them to follow him to the opposite side of the shop, presumably to show them something. It was his misfortune to pass within a yard of Irene who deliberately yet discreetly stuck out her foot to catch his, and caused him the most embarrassing tumble, whereupon he quickly recovered, then turned and apologised to Irene.

Irene's face had the imperturbability of a lump of steel. A great wave of speculative thought passed over the couple's faces. We could have walked out then, but our desperation was clearly outstripping our pride, for we continued to wait. In any case, I thought, the British Raj had never before turned to run, as far as I'd heard, and this was no time to begin a new experiment. Perhaps it was the whole embarrassing incident itself that did it, but the man actually bought the drawing with great servility after the couple had departed.

Outside, we soon forgot the tension and once more giggled. "Rupees. Rupees galore!" chortled Irene. And indeed we both felt like millionaires once more, though I cannot remember how much she got, nor can Irene. I discovered on research that Jennie had been in exactly the same monetary predicament after leaving Koggala. We took a trip to a delightful swimming pool straight away, and then to a beach, and what a pleasure it was to get into water again.

We were beginning to think we would never get a ship, and I knew everyone at home was wondering too. I hadn't written and told them how desperately poor we were. I was so newly married, from every point of view it never occurred to me to shout out letter-wise, "Send me some money". Because of course we were still in the Air Force, still supposed to be getting our pay. The trouble was everybody in the hotel seemed to be in the same boat. I suppose I could have sold my watch or jewellery, but that did seem to take things too far. Anyway, each new day brought fresh hope of a ship, though I think we'd have accepted anything that would move us and each morning we talked about it.

Suddenly, however, I was in no more need of money. I was sitting early one morning, and as a Sergeant came past me she stopped and looked. Then she leant towards me: "What's wrong with you?"

"I don't know, it's just started." I knew as well as she did, and she knew it, what my shivering meant. My whole body had been racked with it for about ten minutes, as if I was an advanced case of shell shock. I had the damned fever once more, but the reason I had not rushed to report sick was that I was fearful of missing a ship, should the miracle happen that morning. I'd been sitting thinking about that as far as my shivers would allow. I'd miserably visualised waving Irene off and then having to travel home with strangers.

The Sergeant's voice leapt into an adjoining room: "Richards-Jones (or some such title) come and take this shivering lump of flesh to sick-bay."

I was led to a further room of the hotel that was being used for the continuous stream of the suffering. Irene, who'd been in the bathroom at the time it happened, couldn't understand where I'd got to. That's how suddenly the shivering can strike. It was dengue fever I'd got, which is a sort of relation to yellow fever. In sick-bay each bed had an occupant, and each bed and doorway a net. There was a canvas-covered chair even, for anyone able to sit. It stood beside a small table covered with a pretty cloth on which stood a bowl of flowers. The inevitable black portable was also there to help us while away time.

The riddle of the flowers became obvious, when a high-ranking woman came to inspect us, or alternatively give us sympathy. She had the meticulous style needed to go around giving succour to the troops and came and complimented me on my hairstyle, which was nothing really. I had simply taken it over my head in two plaits because it had grown so long, and the innovation had been to a further effort to keep cool, once the shivering had passed.

I was released from sick-bay and need not have worried because still there was no ship for me. Then Irene and I were lucky to get the company of two RAF boys for two weeks. They turned out to be splendid dancers and paid us into a hall for the troops. There was even quite a good band. Some days we went swimming with them too.

When we'd quite decided that all knowledge of our existence had been forgotten, and we'd become simply two lost documents of the Empire, the astounding news came one morning that if we really hurried and packed, they might let us on a ship, only "might" we were warned.

It was a picture of "who flung what" or "who flung that" as kit bags were feverishly stuffed regardless this time of valuables. We arrived at the docks with the distinct feeling that they'd probably already left without us, had decided at the last minute we were still too unimportant for this one.

So it was with an even greater surprise that we not only found the ship waiting, but in fact it was our former home that we had sailed out on. It was the good old *Johann Van Olden Barneveldt*. Our dear old friend had obligingly come to our rescue. We stood on the dock and jumped for joy, beaming from ear to ear.

CHAPTER
NINETEEN

No, Dear, I Didn't Get Pregnant!

Irene and I discovered ourselves among a shipload of people, this time rather different from those of our outward journey. Most of the men seemed somewhat older, certainly less frisky than those on the outgoing voyage. Now, of course, we were mixing with men who'd been away for a few years, men returning with uncertainty about what lay ahead. There was little of the spirit of the outward journey when we'd been a shipload of youngsters mostly, looking forward eagerly then with a great spirit of adventure, to a world of new horizons.

Now the horizons had been viewed, and there was no talk of what they'd seen. The men seemed to play cards a lot, much more than those going out. I don't think any of us had yet come to terms with the idea that now the war was ended, we could go ahead and ask questions. I did in fact wonder why a bunch of Canadians were aboard. One of them certainly seemed as if he expected to be in Britain for a while, for he was looking for an invitation when he got there. But neither

Irene nor I were in a position to invite anybody anywhere. I hardly knew myself where I'd be going, now that I was no longer single.

However, the Canadian was attractive, charming, so when he was taken ill on board Irene and I were pleased to visit him in the sickroom, which seemed to please him enormously. We took him grapes from the shop and sat and ate them with him.

Irene said nothing about what her moves would be on her return either. I suppose we both had the idea in mind first of all that our mothers would be longing to see us. True or not, that's where we went. But still aboard, we spent some of the long hours recalling the months since we'd left West Kirby, what it had meant to us both; and we promised ourselves, whilst gazing at some rosy path that lay ahead, that someday, sometime in the new uncertain future, we would get together again and take a trip across the Mediterranean. We felt we could not travel through life without seeing again the sights we had so enjoyed. We still had no idea that having been born a woman, life was waiting to snare us. We had both taken the first step on that less than rosy road. I had married, Irene was proposing to marry again. Marriage meant children. Children meant a trap.

Men usually word it another way. They claim woman is the trap, but in reality they enjoy woman, and only when children come do they see woman as such. Irene was in fact to discover that men are never trapped, more fully than the rest of us discover it.

We reached Southampton in November. It took just two days to demobilise me, or much less considering the time I spent in an office getting my papers. That was five minutes. I was invited to take a seat at a desk, by a Sergeant, or perhaps he was a flight. He made little impression on me.

"Now you'll need a reference," he said, in a voice so casual, I felt I'd just been charring for a few weeks. I stared at him questioningly, and he stared back at me likewise.

"Well, do you think something like this will be suitable?" he asked, then went on, "Mm, something like — Has a very sound knowledge of her trade, a keen and reliable worker, recommended for a position as a secretary to any well-established firm. Eh?"

"Yes, I suppose so," I answered, so that is what he wrote.

I felt that anything either of us said at that moment would be inadequate. How *does* one sum up a small lifetime? And somebody was suddenly asking me a question I hardly knew how to answer, even on such a vital point. Yet pre-war, people in the office had never stopped asking me questions. Suddenly I just saw mysclf as 2092336.

I questioned Jennie as to what happened to her on release.

"Oh, I had an interview with the Commanding Officer. Quite a long talk in fact." He'd even asked her what her plans were.

I felt very much that I'd got the boot, but of course I'm sure even our officers felt a little the same. The truth was that war had landed us in a rut and now we were all struggling to get out, and what would we find when we got ourselves free?

However, I am still at a loss to understand how their system of promotion worked — how one ex-WAAF had gained corporal's stripes, yet I still just had my props. I had been graded higher than her for work proficiency. She was classed as just satisfactory, and I was classed as superior. We had exactly the same length of service, and neither of us had lost on bad conduct of any sort. I'm still grinding my teeth over that.

I travelled by train from Southampton to the north. The other occupants of the carriage were also showing shades of having spent a long time in the sun, and their chatter was all about their experiences. My thoughts were on Gordon. I didn't know where he was stationed, and it occurred to me if I had known I might have been able to visit him. Yet I was loaded with luggage, and also perhaps he was at home. I barely wavered from the idea I must simply go there. That would be what everyone expected of me.

The journey was absolutely appalling, the train strangely empty in contrast to the war years. No jolly servicemen to share the travel time with. A male civilian in our carriage seemed to be viewing us already like something from another world.

I had landed in England when snow had been on the ground for some time. It was cold, wet, dirty snow. It and the damp temperature were disagreeable in the extreme. Almost colder than when I'd left England. The backs of houses as we passed them looked dismal and very shabby, just as if a war had been going on. There was only dullness, greyness, and a lustreless sky. What favoured birth they had in the east I began to think. All those blue skies. But I'd sent my mother a telegram and she was waiting for me at the station.

I'd eaten nothing the whole of the journey, so she took me into the nearest café to the bus stop, as we'd taken a bus from the station, and there was still another bus to go. We sat and had a cup of tea. I could not face food in the place. The floor of the café was patterned with dirt and wet from the snow. That was excusable, but it was the tabletops that took away my appetite. They all looked as if their greasy tops had been wiped with an equally greasy rag. My first impression on my return to the homeland could not have been more unsightly or any less welcoming. I felt I could have run back east. Back to the sun, back to the cleanliness.

Gordon, who had been eager for my return, was now himself the one to be holding our lives apart still. In fact it was several more months before he got his release. The government was wisely avoiding a flooding of the work market; a lesson that had been learned in the aftermath of the 1914–18 war.

Had I known how long it would take for him to get his release, I might well have taken a job, but I kept expecting him every week, in the same way we'd waited for a ship in India. And the social system I'd been brought up in led me to believe I should be ready and waiting for my husband's return.

My sister-in-law was now sharing our home with her young son, so that there were too many female hands running one house. My brother was also still away.

However, it was nice to have money in my purse again. Gordon in fact had ordered an allowance to be paid to me in England as soon as we'd been married, thinking I'd apply and be sent there immediately, but as you heard things did not work out like that.

There was a communication waiting for me to tell me of the allowance that was being paid at the Post Office, and the bulk of several months was waiting for me. When I answered the letter by appearing in person, the counter assistant asked: "Where on earth have you been? Don't you need your allowance?"

I explained the mystery to him, wondering how he had not noticed my suntan in the middle of winter. All he said was "Oh."

I was released from service on the 8th January 1946. When my old firm heard of my release they sent for me. I was pleased to discover they had a number of saving certificates on my behalf so that in the end, we had enough cash to buy ourselves furniture without any skimping, for we also had a gratuity each to add to that. It was better than nothing for four and a half years away from home, though it was quite a while before we got a house of our own.

However, the sort of thing that seems to make war meaningless and proves they'll never alter people, happened on my visit to my old office. I had a pleasant talk with my ex-bosses, the younger one of whom sadly died from tuberculosis in South Africa not long after. He had asked me to return to my job saying he'd never had any decent girls since we'd left. I thought that was a great compliment to the three of us, Jean, Jennie and myself. I told him I'd think about it, because I no longer lived in the area of course, and had no idea where I'd end up living. It was then he informed me that Winnie had returned to her job there. I felt he was holding this out as a carrot almost. I knew Winnie had also joined the WAAFs later than us. He suggested I have a word with her if I wished.

I'd known her since school days so immediately went to renew our acquaintance. I'd heard too that she had married a Polish airman, which had made me laughingly wonder if it was mine at Cranwell.

"Hello, it's nice to see you," she commented on my entering her office.

"Thanks," I replied, and before I could say more she continued. Her next words astounded me. "You don't look very pregnant to me!" She was looking me up and down, while I stood before her in a very close-fitting brown velour coat, which I'd been delighted to find fitted me just as well as a few years before.

I must have gaped at her, and I remember saying "What d'you mean?" quite sharply in fact.

"Oh, well, they're saying that's why you got married so suddenly."

I could hardly believe my ears. I was fuming inwardly. I had been away all that time — it had felt like a lifetime — and it seemed that just because I'd done something, which it seemed obvious they hadn't approved of, they had concocted some illegitimate reason for it. I felt disgusted with the human race. I thought with a wave of bitterness, "I've been away fighting their war for them, and look how far the minds of my old village have advanced. Not one bloody iota!" I felt actually glad my mother had moved from the place, had gone to the city and left the village idiots behind.

"Then I suggest you run back and tell them, whoever it is, how damn wrong they are!" I told her.

They had suddenly made me into a swearing monster, and I heartily wished Mr Percy had not suggested my visit. I looked at the puzzled face before me wondering why she too, ex-grammar school, was muddling along with the rest of them. Had she not learnt anything by going away? It seemed the old die-hards were still at it, still demeaning life to their own fearful level. Heaven forbid that I should ever join them again I thought. I never went back to the office.

I remember what Pearl said to me. She was an ex-WAAF who'd been introduced to me with regard to this book. I thought her story was very interesting. She confessed she'd been utterly spoilt at home. A singularly doted-upon child. Her parents had belonged in a narrow sense to one religion. Pearl had been called to do war service. She'd joined the WAAFs but unlike most, had asked to be a wireless operator, and had become one of the "Bentley Priory hundreds".

Her mother had sent her half-a-crown each week, and the same to her friend she had in the service, who says she never forgot the kindness, particularly as she came from a poor — in the money sense — background.

We had a most interesting afternoon and managed to pull a lot from one another, and at the end we had both come to a very definite conclusion. We had used our own experience to come to it in a large sense too, that all children should be sent or taken from their parents before some of the stigmas are absorbed, to a degree where they are difficult to obliterate. Perhaps then we would have many less wars. But then of course, where do we find the specials that would bring up the children in an unbiased way? I must spend an afternoon again with Pearl.

It was interesting too that Pearl had known for twenty-four hours before anybody else when war came to an end. She told me: "I actually read the signal as it came onto the teleprinter at Bentley Priory. I've never understood why it took so long to be announced publicly. I was dying to tell somebody; but of course I didn't dare."

"Then despite being a spoilt young lady, you enjoyed your time in the WAAFs?" I asked.

Pearl replied: "Yes indeed. It made a new person of me. One I'm sure I like much better than the one I might have been."

I think that is a statement that could be true of many an ex-WAAF. Surprisingly, not one of the WAAFs I've spoken to ever thought of applying for the medals to which they were entitled. I only decided to apply for mine when I'd made up my mind to write my story. Yes, they still had them waiting for me, but by now showing the slightest of tarnish. How many thousands more remain, unclaimed, from Records at Gloucester. I think this point gives proof undeniably, how we all underestimated our worth in winning our war — highly underestimated our worth. Perhaps they will send them all off one day to make room for the next war's prizes.

While I was impatiently waiting for Gordon to come home I kept a promise. After I'd written to tell Eric the rotten news for him, he had written and asked to see me just once more, telling me it was the least I owed him. I felt he was right, one cannot just end such an association with a letter. I'd be able to explain better face to face, or so I thought.

I had business in Leeds and promised to meet him there. Although I was at first against it, we travelled from there down to his home, for he told me his mother would expect me. They welcomed me as if I was an angel who had done no wrong and made me feel very humble. They'd been stout friends in war, and intended to remain friends in peace, despite my decision. Perhaps they felt in some way they wanted to repay me, for I always remember Eric's mother once saying: "I'm very proud of you. Dennis has told me of the secret work you must do, yet you have never once breathed anything about it to us. Bless you for that." I'd never thought of it that way myself.

When my first child was born they sent me gifts, and later, quite a lot later, it was I, not they, who stopped writing. Not from reluctance to do so, but for the same reason Irene and I never took that Mediterranean Cruise, because life drained me of time, and once the gap got so long in writing it was difficult to find the initiative again. And the same must have happened to them too. Indeed the last letter I remember receiving, was to tell me his father was dying, but his sister asked me not to mention it in my next letter because their mother did not know. I remember trying to write a letter, which I hoped, would help to cheer them.

Irene got her problem sorted and married Harry on one of his leaves, but sadly, a few spans later, which included two infants, Harry just disappeared from her life and was not heard of again. She was expecting him home for his demob leave, but he never turned up. She told me, many years later:

"Only my mother saved me from a mental breakdown. You know, I've had the same dream every night since then. I see Harry waiting for me on the beach at Koggala. Isn't that funny?"

Jennie didn't come straight home. She took up work away and met her husband, and then came home again. She had a daughter. Jean never came home. She married and like myself had both a son and daughter. She comes to visit her sister-in-law though, and has promised to meet me again since I phoned her about the book. Sadly, she is now a widow, so I cannot meet the man who eventually won her, the man who gave her the best compliment of all.

It will take a long talk to catch up so many years. Of course now we all have time again, for all our children are grown and leading independent lives. And that too is why I have at last been able to put down this story. A little part of a mighty war but a true account nevertheless, of one or two of the many

Lambs in Blue — those lesser ranks who, for a long time, have kept their mouths shut about what they did. You must remember them, boys!

Postscript

I dedicated this book to the boys who flew, and still do, but I feel it is very important to point out that WAAFs were also injured and killed in the war.

Of the thousands who joined, few of us got the chance to be real heroines, yet each girl worked unstintingly, often in bitter cold, and in our case extreme heat also. I never heard one complain, unless in fun, the simple reason being we were most of us so young. It was truly the very youth of Britain who shone like a beacon, did so much, and were paid so little for it. We girls got two-thirds of men's wages for some strange reason.

None of us were ever glad about the war, we weren't so silly. But like Pearl, many of us learnt to live happily with strangers. We learnt of the world beyond our own door, of the various social levels and trappings of our society. But, however I look back at it, one things stands out; when the majority of us left home and first put on that uniform which became so well known, we were truthfully, very young, very innocent, very much a bunch of *Lambs in Blue*.

The operations rooms are still underground, empty now of our machines and vital messages, but for us all, still the haunts of young girls; some charming, some naughty, many just faithfully sticking to duty.

I'd hunted maps for the name Koggala, but could never find it as I wrote, yet it had been so real. Then just as I was on the last chapter Jennie came rushing across one day.

"Look," she yelled, "You'll never believe it. I've found it."

"What," I asked cautiously, knowing her enthusiasm, "have you found?"

"Koggala. Actually written on a map." She showed me a holiday brochure from Cosmos telling everyone to "GO EAST".

And there it was, just as she'd said. Not only that, it showed us a picture, and underneath it said: "Koggala Beach Hotel". I got a funny little excited feeling, but I also wondered: "What have they done to our jungle? I bet they've gone and cleared it all away." I didn't like the thought of that.

"We must go back," said Jennie.

"But will it be the same?" I asked.

We gave one another a look that is impossible to describe.

ISIS publish a wide range of books in large print, from fiction to biography. Any suggestions for books you would like to see in large print or audio are always welcome. Please send to the Editorial department at:

ISIS Publishing Ltd.
7 Centremead
Osney Mead
Oxford OX2 0ES
(01865) 250 333

A full list of titles is available free of charge from:
Ulverscroft large print books

(UK)
The Green
Bradgate Road, Anstey
Leicester LE7 7FU
Tel: (0116) 236 4325

(Australia)
P.O Box 953
Crows Nest
NSW 1585
Tel: (02) 9436 2622

(USA)
1881 Ridge Road
P.O Box 1230, West Seneca,
N.Y. 14224-1230
Tel: (716) 674 4270

(Canada)
P.O Box 80038
Burlington
Ontario L7L 6B1
Tel: (905) 637 8734

(New Zealand)
P.O Box 456
Feilding
Tel: (06) 323 6828

Details of **ISIS** complete and unabridged audio books are also available from these offices. Alternatively, contact your local library for details of their collection of **ISIS** large print and unabridged audio books.